BRITAIN IN OLD PHOTOGRAPHS

# WELWYN
# GARDEN CITY

MARION HILL

SUTTON PUBLISHING LIMITED

Sutton Publishing Limited
Phoenix Mill · Thrupp · Stroud
Gloucestershire · GL5 2BU

First published 1999

*Title page photograph*: 'Landscaping for the
Commission for the New Towns, 1969'
(CNT R/1631/7A).

**British Library Cataloguing in Publication Data**
A catalogue record for this book is available from the
British Library.

ISBN 0-7509-2004-1

Typeset in 10.5/13.5 Photina.
Typesetting and origination by
Sutton Publishing Limited.
Printed in Great Britain by
Ebenezer Baylis, Worcester.

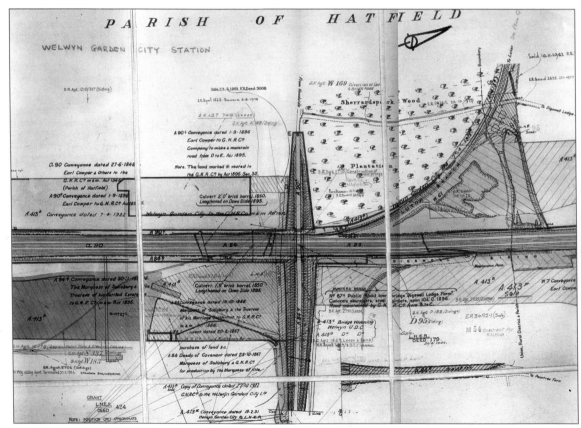

Conveyances for part of the Welwyn Garden City (WGC) station area from 1848 to 1984 (*Railtrack Property*). This historic map has been overwritten with railway property deals covering 136 years. They include the original conveyance of 27.6.1848 with 'Earl Cowper and others' (left); 'No. 67A Public Road over bridge "Digswell Lodge Farm". . . . Concrete abutments, steel girders, span 104 ft, 1896' – alias Hunters Bridge (centre right); and 'BR siding agreement terminated 30.3.1984' (bottom left).

# CONTENTS

The 'Lion' train, used for the film *The Lady with the Lamp* starring Anna Neagle, 1951. 'The train was built in 1838 and had been borrowed from Lime Street Station, Liverpool where it has been kept. . . . Both the driver and fireman used in the film are local men, "borrowed" for the occasion. They were Mr H. Page of 40 Park Street and Mr E. Hazelwood of 18 Ethelred Close, Welwyn Garden City, who normally drive a modern train on the local line' (*Welwyn Times – WT*). Ted Hazelwood (standing on the engine) recalls: *It was brought on a wagon as far as Hertford. My driver and I went to Hertford, helped unload it on to what was then the Hatfield–Hertford–Welwyn Garden City branch line to Cole Green station.*

\* The verbatim words of contributors to this book are shown throughout in italics.

The Welwyn Stores, 1929 (*courtesy Ann Adams*). The Stores were the Welwyn Garden City Company's flagship monopoly. Despite its many businesses, the Company (WGCC) was in voluntary liquidation by 1949.

'Occasion of the visit of officials from the Commission for the New Towns (CNT) to WGC at the time of the Development Corporation (WGCDC) being wound up: C. Gordon Maynard, WGCDC Chairman and Sir Henry Wells, CNT Chairman, 28 March 1966' (*CNT 75/11/1219/20*). WGCDC had been designated in 1948 for one of the first new towns of the post-war era; one of its first acts was to buy WGCC in September 1949. After its hand-over to CNT in 1966, CNT itself transferred WGC assets to the Welwyn Hatfield District Council (WHDC) in 1978.

# PROLOGUE

1st Labourer: Wot's this Bill?
2nd Labourer: Woi! It's a gorden city.
1st Labourer: Wot's a gorden city?
2nd Labourer: Don't yer know? Woi! It's a plice where all the loidies wear no shoes or stockings, all the 'ouses 'ave tin roofs and everyboidy keeps a goat. . . .

This exchange was apparently overheard by 'a well-known Director of Welwyn Garden City as the train approached Letchworth', according to the first edition of *The Welwyn Garden City and Hatfield Pilot* in September 1922, just as Britain's second Garden City was under way. Les Westlake's first memories of the area certainly asserted its rustic dimension: *It was lovely coming down from London, coming down to all those fields to wander through. My mother came down to oil lamps, coal fires, a kitchen range for cooking and outside sanitation.* However, a 1829 poem by Theodore Hook, quoted by the WGCC in its 1930 book for new residents, suggested a more ethereal connection:

> You ask me where in peaceful grot
> I'd choose to fix my dwelling,
> I'll tell you; for I've found the spot,
> And mortals call it Welwyn. . . .

The family featured in *The Magic Train*, a children's book compiled by Lisa Sheridan, 1930 (*Bodley Head*). In real life, they were the children and wife (Marjorie) of Councillor Wyvil August of Dellcott Close. Mrs August was sister to Captain W.E. James, the Engineer for the original WGCC which created the town.

Unfortunately, the 'spot' about which Hook had waxed poetic was, in fact, the little village just to the north of the new Garden City designated area but there was an appealingly bucolic charm in the names of ancient settlements of the area – 'Welga', 'Welewe', 'Willen', 'Wellinge' all reportedly meant 'at the willows'. As it was, the search for a final name produced a spirited debate: residents of the village of Welwyn reacted strongly both to being lumped in with the new town and to being fobbed off as 'Old Welwyn'; a distinction had to be made. Suggestions included Welwyn South, Welwyn Wood, Welwynhyde, Welwynhurst, Welwyndune, Welwynhoo, and Welwyngard. More ambitious were Welwynvented, Welwyntentioned, Welcomewyn and Sweet Smelwyn. . . .

Of course, Ebenezer Howard had had his sights set on more than naming: *I went into some of the crowded parts of London . . . as I passed through the narrow dark streets, I saw the wretched dwellings in which the majority of people lived, observed on every hand the manifestations of a self-seeking order and reflected on the absolute unsoundness of our economic system . . . the entire unsuitability (of the environment) for the working life of the new order – that of justice, unity and friendliness.* As has been well documented, a Garden City was his means to the end of abolishing slums and unemployment, nothing less than building a new civilisation. On Friday 30 May 1919 he *bought 1,458 acres of land for £51,000 without the cash to pay for it* (Sir Frederic Osborn). Death duties had forced the Desborough family to sell off the Panshanger farms, Digswell House and park, Handside Upper and Lower farms, Brickwall Farm, 'Digswellwater' Farm, Black Fan and Sherrards Wood; and Howard's new Welwyn Garden City Company Ltd won the auction.

   Just one year later in the 'birth-year' of the new town, 1920, *the first trenches were cut and the first bricks laid. (Then) the Company issued its prospectus and went to allotment. I cannot describe, even list the multitude of problems we had to tackle in the year before building began. Big books have been*

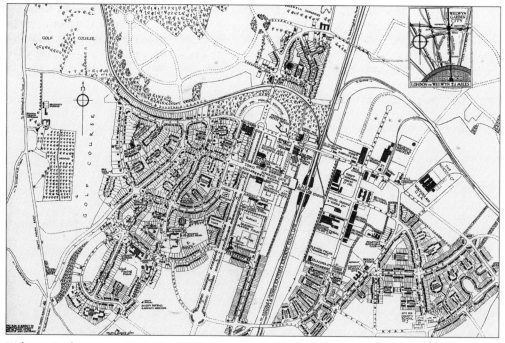

Welwyn Garden City map, 1929 (*courtesy Ann Adams*). Freda Schaschke, who kept the Citizens' Guide containing this map when she lived in the Garden City in about 1930, marked on it where she lived in Dognell Green (centre left), where she would play tennis (just above), and where she worked as a nanny to Major Povak's family in Digswell Road (top centre).

*written on them and probably some day fatter ones will be written by patient Guggenheim or Rockefeller scholars* (Osborn). The area covered four parishes and three rural districts – *2,300 acres . . . in an almost uninhabited rural area with only a few farm cottages, a few lengths of mainly unmetalled road, no railway station nearer than Welwyn North and Hatfield, and no services such as main drainage, water, gas and electricity* (R.L. Reiss).

A great deal of hard work was done in the early years but there was no equivalent interest in the Garden City outside it. The Company highlighted weekly advertisements in its newspaper, the *WGC Times* (*WGCT*), on the housing and environmental attributes of WGC, with an element of desperation. In December 1926 the Company Chairman, Sir Theodore Chambers, expressed his frustration in an 'acrimonious and invective harangue': *It is very difficult to be patient. . . . WGC has reached its present state in six years in the face of apathy, scepticism and unbelief* (*WGCT*).

Despite early financial problems the Garden City thrived: at first, *social energy was released at its highest power; barriers of class and income were for the time being ignored. . . . Everybody without exception went to the same meetings and functions, to the same religious meetings, political discussions, dances, social gatherings, tennis parties, amateur plays, impromptu concerts. . . . There was no established social hierarchy to thwart people's spontaneous friendliness* (Osborn). The Welwyn Times claimed in 1930: 'One of the most distinctive characteristics of Welwyn Garden City as a community is that it possesses more societies to the square inch than any other place of its size.' The 75 organisations listed offered Garden City residents unlimited opportunities for educational, literary, linguistic, artistic, sporting, hygienic and horticultural development: everything from philanthropy to tiddlywinks.

The WGCC's main thrust was of course in construction: it employed 1,000 people in its building operations alone; indeed, at least half the population in 1928 (7,000) were employed by the Company in its various businesses. However, most were housed in dwellings built by the company for the local authority (the Rural District Council) to standards laid down in the Housing Act of 1919 – in other words 'council houses' – and most of these were built on the eastern side of the railway. It was this perhaps more than anything that made WGC into a 'hornet's nest to Socialism'. George Bernard Shaw denounced them as 'slums'; they were 'literally a class apart from the superior properties advertised by the company as good investment'. One trade unionist in 1928 dismissed WGC as 'bourgeois villadom, irrelevant to the needs of working class people'. In 1937 this poem was written by 'AW' in the *Welwyn Times* in response to a letter about the formal dress requirement at a Council function:

> This royal home of cranks, this bearded town,
> This barber's curse, this seat of Marx,
> This other Bloomsbury, this demi-paradise;
> This fortress built by Howards for us all
> Against infection by the bourgeoisie...
> This land of such wet souls, this dear (very dear) land
> Is now leased out like unto Saville Row. . . .
>
> Garden City, bound in by the triumphant woods,
> Is now bound with shame
> With stiff shirt fronts, tail-coats and Golf Club Routs
> And Coronation Balls
> And Councillors in lounge suits turned away.
> So quick, bright things come to confusion.

For ordinary Garden Citizens, the issue was more basic: *Welwyn Stores was the only shop as everything belonged to Welwyn Garden City Ltd, including the bakery, laundry, builders etc. so with no competition it was an expensive place in which to live* (WI member).

Notwithstanding the grumbles, the WGCC continually asserted its principle of a quality environment for all: 'WGC is not a fancy product, an expensive luxury for a few epicures. On the contrary, it is firmly rooted in economic realities. It has had to satisfy normal workday demands.

Its houses have to be comfortable and within the means of people of all classes, including weekly wage-earners who work in the town, and professional and business men and retired people who are attracted by it as a place of residence. What is being done at Welwyn has practical value for the world in these days when both town and country are being spoiled on a wholesale scale by ugly and ill-considered building. Ugliness is unnecessary. It saves nothing. It is due simply to lack of forethought and lack of reasonable control' (Preface to Citizens' Handbook, 1930).

Louis de Soissons had been appointed Town Planner and Architect in 1920: *it is very much his town, like Parisian boulevards and the Tuileries Gardens. The predominant style is a quiet, comfortable neo-Georgian with De Soissons' favourite round window like a mason's mark on houses of different types and sizes. Curving streets dominate. No more inspiring task can be imagined than the provision for millions of our people of the best physical environment that modern art and industry can produce* (Osborn). Indeed, Sir Ebenezer Howard's maxim for the Garden City has been a key to New Town planning ever since: '[It is] not a district at the mercy of every kind of haphazard building development, but an ordered town in which the fitness of each building for its site is considered. No jerry building is permitted (*The Alphabetical Guide to WGC*, 1927). Similarly, *the Corporation ruled with a fist of iron. In order to preserve the dream of the founder, it was necessary to keep WGC as neat as it started out. They had to make sure that people did not spoil the look of the town. There were many rules for tenants: the garden had to be kept neat and tidy; we were not allowed to rig up any old hut for tools; [even] the roof of a shed had to have a predetermined colour of roofing felt* (Helga Lomas).

*For WGC children, it was the sense of freedom which appealed: the first few years were wonderful. There was the excitement of new houses being built, space to play, woods to roam in, trees to climb . . . a great team of experts, idealists, directors and workmen were going to build the ideal planned city: everything had to be started new. My father, who seemed to be the centre of leadership in everything, took me round with him. Here was a deep well for pumping water, here clay was dug and bricks shaped and cooked in kilns; there were sidings to serve great new factories, here were the huts where workmen lived, brains thought, clerks administered, people worshipped; here was a shed called 'Bank' to get money. That field where men played cricket would be a shopping centre, and those muddy places and deep timber strutted trenches were to be clean dry roads and underground drainage* (Richard Reiss).

'Up the mountain, Ludwick, 1950' (*Miss Smith, courtesy Joan Lammiman*).

# CHAPTER ONE

# HATFIELD HYDE & THE SOUTH-EAST

The climbing tree at Ludwick Infants School, Peartree, 1950 *(Miss Smith, courtesy Joan Lammiman). Seventy years ago the eastern side of town was known to us on the western side simply as 'Peartree' and was thought of as 'lower class' (though goodness knows what we had to be uppish about). But we were children of our time and we unconsciously absorbed this piece of snobbery from our elders and thought it a normal attitude, so 'Peartree kids' were regarded as our natural enemies. Just occasionally there would be a pitched battle in Sherrards Wood between the two factions, but the weapons were usually no more than words (Alec Scott).*

The south-east area is the largest of the four main sections of the town. At its centre there used to be 'a typical Hertfordshire village', Hatfield Hyde, in its day also the largest community in the area. It had two pubs, The Woodman (now The Chieftain) which had the longest bar in the county; and The Beehive. It had a war memorial at George's Corner and a little church, St Mary Magdalene's. It had around 80 eponymous dwellings including the stately sounding Hyde House and Ludwick Hall, and the modestly named Richardson's cottages, The Flint Cottage, The Row cottages and Sandpit cottages – where no. 1 was Mrs Welch's sub-post office; and Mrs Granny Birch's sweet shop was packed with liquorice pipes and braids, sherbet bags, gob-stoppers, whatohs, chocolate creams, fudges and boiled sweets.

One resident remembers it as *a peaceful little place, and in the summer when the fields were a mass of gold buttercups, daisies, and ripe corn blowing in the breeze, it was very beautiful. . . . [There were] wild roses growing in the hedges and apple blossom on trees in the cottage gardens. . . . The local farmers always allowed us to go gleaning in the cornfields* [the painstaking collection of individual heads of corn left on the ground after harvesting]. *Sometimes we collected enough to feed the hens all the winter* ('RT'). Another recalls: *I was born in Hatfield Hyde in a house in a dusty old lane near the Woodman pub, a cottage pub. I was there until I was 4 years old. I can remember when I was about 3 (in 1917), sitting on the side of the road with my father, watching the aeroplanes circling in the 1914–18 war. I remember a big bang too – they dropped a bomb in Brocket Park, a Zeppelin that was. When the Zeppelins came over, all the pheasants used to squawk! They made a heck of a noise* (Walter Broughton).

Mr and Mrs Cooper outside The Flint Cottage, Hatfield Hyde, *c.* 1910 (courtesy *Joan Lammiman*). This farmworker's cottage was attached to the Peartree Farm estate. It was demolished in 1938 when the Woodhall area began to develop.

'Aerial of the Hospital site (top right) and St Mary Magdalene, 1957' (*CNT C/16.961/B*). King George V Playing Fields are above the church with the new developments of Howlands (right), Mountway and Ryelands (centre) and The Wade (top centre left). The first church and school in the WGC area was the Mud Chapel, used also as a library, medical club, and for craft classes. *It closed in 1932, then it became a mattress factory. In 1945 it caught fire (the roof fell in and with it the bell), then it was pulled down. A building was put on top, used as a Guide and Scout hut – it's all gone now. You can still see the floor of it* (Joan Lammiman). In 1972 children found a rusted bell round the back of St Mary's and the following history explaining the bell's provenance unfolded. . . .

The Mud Chapel, 1861–1946, which housed Hatfield Hyde CE School from 1875 to 1932, drawn in 1973 by Valerie Gibbons, a teacher at the school (*courtesy Joan Lammiman*). The last Mud Chapel Headmistress, Miss Poppy Swift, started as a monitor at the age of 14 in 1902. The log books record hanging curtains to divide the room (1907); closing school because bad weather had made the children too wet (1910); and 4 weeks' holiday for children to help with the potato harvest (1916). At its peak the roll was 106. There were long, hard wooden benches, slates, ink-wells and dip pens, a tortoise stove, a rough wooden floor swept with tea-leaves, primitive toilets across the playground, water from the well across the lane, and a bell that called the children to school. . . .

'The Hyde Association's new Community Centre showing the original Hyde House before its demolition, 1967' (*CNT P/1658/19*). Next to St Mary Magdalene, the house was home to Mrs Georgiana Kendall, a Governor of the Mud Chapel School: *How we hated meeting her in the village, because we had to curtsey to her. If we did not, she would come down to the school, call us out and make us apologise to her* ('RT'). *When Mrs Gurney lived there, we used to camp there and keep stuff in the stables* (Derek Greener). *It was already fairly dilapidated when I went to Keep Fit classes there in the early 1960s. We used to sit upstairs, always afraid that we might fall through. The floorboards were very creaky!* (Dorothea Bagge).

'Church of St Mary Magdalene, 1957' (*CNT G/JC/DC20*). Built in 1883 to replace the Mud Chapel, the church was heated by a 'large cylindrical-shaped coke-burning combustion stove, and lit by candles and paraffin lamps'. *We were married at St Mary Magdalene (1953). It was lovely. Now they've put that terrible annexe on it. It was a tiny little church. On our wedding day, it rained. Ted's mum was a cook at the British Restaurant (up Heronswood Road, where the fire station is now). We had our wedding reception in there. You had to beg, borrow and steal coupons for it* (Anne Hazelwood).

'Aerial of the South East – Hatfield Hyde I, 25.2.1954' (*CNT A/12182/B*). The site of the hospital is top left, bounded by Ascots Lane (centre left) and Howlands (left centre to top right). The Wade (foreground) is nearing completion.

'Aerial of Hospital under construction, June 1962' (*CNT M/25036/A*). The railway crosses the top of the picture, left to right; King George V Playing Fields are centre above The Wade, with Beehive Lane curving from right centre. Howlands runs from top left to bottom right.

'Visit of HM Queen Elizabeth II to WGC 22.7.63 to perform the opening ceremony of the new hospital' (*CNT 74/6/417-13*). *When the Queen came to open the Hospital, the council wouldn't supply flags and Barbara Cartland brought them* (Derek Greener). It was the first full-scale hospital to be completed after the war. Work started on its 22-acre site in 1958. Twenty years later it saw the end of an era when WGC's last formal link with the original company that created it in 1920 was lost: Sir Frederic Osborn, its secretary, died at the hospital at the age of 93.

'Howlands in 1968 showing kerbside parking' (*CNT S/1278/18*). *All down Howlands and Heronswood (in the 1950s) were still country except for the main roads. I tried to learn to ride a bike, but was too nervous of the traffic which was so little against today* (Mrs Gann).

'Aerial of Thistle Grove completed 26.6.1957' (*CNT C/16.959/B*). Holwell Hyde Farm is bottom right; the Hertford branch line, now defunct, runs across the top of the picture; Caponfield leads off left centre. Ted and Anne Hazelwood remember pea- and potato-picking in the field now covered by Thistle Grove: *You had to, with the school, during the war. We used to walk from Ethelred Close to here, because there were all wild strawberries down here. We used to bring a bottle of lemonade and a few jam sandwiches. There was a gang of seven or eight of us. Kids used to walk in them days! The day we moved in to our own house (in Thistle Grove), it was lovely. The houses had proper kitchens with cupboards in, and a modern bathroom upstairs.*

'Interior, 82 Caponfield, July 1955' (CNT C/MT/1246). *We'd have spotted dick. We'd sit at the table grating the suet. It would be in a floured cloth and dumped in a pot. That put weight on you! My mum used to make one on a Sunday – no sugar, you'd have it with gravy on it. If there was any over, you'd have it with treacle. They were good fillers. You had margarine and 'best butter'. I still do things like scraping all the butter off the paper. You'd leave it folded up and put it on a pudding* (Anne Hazelwood). *You'd have a tiny piece of corn-beef in a casserole with carrots, suet crusts with onions. You didn't ever go hungry. . . . My mum was so thrilled when she went to drink water from a tap – a sink and a tap in the house!* (Handside Neighbours Club).

'Interior, 82 Caponfield, July 1955' (*CNT C/MT1249*). *We never had a television. We had one living room. So we used to sit at the table and do things. You'd do jigsaws or cutting up. You made your own things – a lot more creative. You had bits of coloured paper and just made do – you'd cut pictures out of the paper. The living room was about 12 feet square. You had the fireplace and just one armchair each side and then the table and the chairs round it* (Anne Hazelwood).

'Interior July 1955, Great Gannett' (*CNT C/MT1245*). Wartime exigencies included *bread-and-milk – the bread cut into squares with sugar and warm milk poured on top. That's what we'd have for breakfast when there wasn't any money or there wasn't any cereal. We'd have porridge, and shredded wheat, but that was expensive. You'd tip water in the soap powder to get it all out. We made banana spread – it was mashed potato with a little bit of banana essence. We had no bananas, so we didn't know what they tasted like* (Anne Hazelwood).

'Aerial of SE Area, 25.5.1954' (*CNT A/12166/B*). The branch line runs across the top by the curve of Great Ganett. Little Ganett is right of centre. *They built the houses in front of a big tip where all the rubbish from London came down! Once, we went there at night-time and there were thousands of rats coming up the railway track. I think we beat the record for getting out of there. Benedictine monks lived behind the Ganetts and could be seen walking around in long brown robes* (Stan Scales). *We moved (to Great Ganett) on 7 March 1953. Half the road was still being built with lots of rubble about. I always say they named the road after me!* (Mrs Gann)

'Aerial of the Cole Green Road, Heronswood, Sweet Briar and Blackthorne School contracts, 30.6.1952' (*CNT B/57/7875/B*). The single track branch line can be seen clearly on the right with the crossing cottage, Holwell Hyde Gatehouse, in the bottom right corner. It became home to Albert Bales when the gatekeeper retired in 1953. Interviewed by a local newspaper in 1988 he said: *This house was built in 1860 on land bought from Lady Cowper. . . . When I first came it had no electricity – we used paraffin lamps. I didn't mind that – they gave a lovely light. Cooking was done with solid fuel and there were four fireplaces in the house. . . . The London rubbish used to come here en route to the tip. Smelt awful!*

'Looking down Sweet Briar, showing part of Hornbeams, April 1955' (*CNT A/RF/10005*). *At Sweet Briar,we used to go blackberrying up there* (Handside Neighbours Club). Rosemary Mitchell remembers *helping make the jelly – the glorious smell of the blackberries cooking – and straining the juice through a muslin bag attached to the legs of an upturned chair . . . glorious smell.* In 1954 a *Welwyn Times* reporter was most impressed with Hornbeams: 'At the foot of this novel building is a long row of cycle sheds . . . and a round tower with many openings between the bricks which houses the dustbins . . . there is not a coal fireplace anywhere (gas fires instead).'

'The Glade, one of the old field ponds off Hall Grove, 1962. WHDC preserved it for the sake of children' (*CNT M/E43*). Unfortunately, this feature does not seem to have survived. Similarly, *a church was built in Hall Grove, but is now an education centre* (Mrs Gann). Mrs G. Murphy, writing to the *Welwyn Times* in 1983 about the area said: *The new building areas become more and more crowded with less and less space, and the whole effect of the town is being spoilt.*

'Hall Grove shopping, 1962' (*CNT K/13597*). Nearby Ludwick Hall was auctioned off in 1954 after the resident of 17 years, a Company Director 'worried by ill-health and complaining of loneliness', was found shot dead by his maid. *My daughter-in-law was born in Ludwick Hall, next to the doctor's surgery – her father bought it. When my son got engaged they had a big party there, in the Hall. They had a swimming pool built there – it was a big place. We had the party out on the grounds. It's still there, but they've built houses in the grounds. An estate agent bought the house in the end and built these houses* (Handside Neighbours Club Member).

'Ludwick Family Club (photo R.W. Kingdon), 1952' (*CNT B/64/PF/7909*). The Ludwick Family Club was opened in 1954. Attached to part of the old house as a joint venture between the Development Corporation and local churches, it was considered the pioneer of community development in later generations of New Towns, when, at the instigation of R.L. Reiss, a full-time social worker who was also a youth leader was appointed to serve the neighbourhood. *The Ludwick Family Club was an old house, there were no shops. One room in the house was a doctor's surgery; another eventually was where we paid our rent* (Mrs Gann).

'Mrs H. Turrell's speech on the occasion of Lady Balniel opening the new children's playground, February 1954' (*CNT 73/19/MC/00372*). A Development Corporation (DC) handout for the day said: 'In an age which is essentially materialistic, it is encouraging to find such close liaison between the religious and the secular.'

'The Ludwick Family Club, May 1955' (*CNT MT/1242*). The Ludwick Arms is on the left of the picture; a day-centre for Old Age Pensioners is on the right. *Where the Ludwick Arms stands was a mass of marguerites which I used to pick and glory in the fact that I now lived almost 'in the country' (Mrs Abbott). The DC owned everything locally and after we had been here a few weeks (in 1953) we had an invitation to a welcoming party in which all the organisations in the Garden City came to meet us. Two men from Little Ganett and one from Great Ganett had converted two barns into our first room for a social (Mrs Gann).*

'New residents at social, February 1954' (*CNT 73/19/8*). *I joined the wives club in 1953 (46 years ago and it's still going strong) and then welcomed new residents. Gradually the club had rooms extending from the old house. There wasn't a church near, so every Sunday the stage became our Church and ministers would come and take a service. The old house was getting dangerous so part had to come down – a small part of it still joins the club. A wonderful man, Arthur Mellard, started the boys' club and stayed many years; it had to fold later because of funds in the Youth Service. The doctor's surgery moved to a new house in Hall Grove; many years later we had the new centre built (Mrs Gann).*

'Basket Making at the Ludwick Family Club, May 1955' (*CNT 75/24/MT/1269*). Young women were particularly well catered for in the Garden City: the YWCA was founded in Ludwick in 1942. According to the WGC Citizen's handbook of 1946, it was 'originally for the transferred war workers; membership (in 1946) includes mixed Youth Group, YWCA Club, Trevelyan House, open every day for light refreshments, lounge, indoor games, evening classes, dances, outings etc.' Younger girls were kept busy too: the Ludwick Way Girls' Life Brigade activities included 'PT (physical training), First Aid, Handicrafts, Singing, Elocution, and Country Dancing'.

'Puppet Making at Ludwick, May 1955' (*CNT 75/24/MT/1266*). In the same week that the Ludwick Boys Club announced it was full, the *Welwyn Times* reported the case of a gang of 6 'Knella boys': 'We get fed up at weekends just walking around together. We seemed to be at a loose end and didn't know what we were doing.' Over three years one of them had stolen '9 Swiss files, 61 drills, 4 screwdrivers, 4 pairs of pliers, 8 spanners, 14 hacksaw blades, 28 taps, 6 paint-brushes, 3 Abrafiles, 2 broaching levers, and 9 split dies, a total value £13 17*s* 9*d*', all taken from Murphy Radio where he had been employed; he was sent to Borstal. As the judge called them 'a vulgar gang of little boys', one of the mothers broke down and was carried from the court (1954).

'The Cubs and Brownies guard of honour for Mrs Duncan Sandys at the opening of Ludwick Launderette 1955' (*CNT 75/20/MT/1199*). The *Welwyn Times* reported: 'Spick and span [they] had their reward when Mrs Sandys had a charming word with each child, asking his or her name . . . extracting a promise from the press photographer to take pictures of all the little children.' *My daughter was a Brownie (and) part of the Guard of Honour when the Sandys came to open the laundry. The laundry was successful for a while, but in the end did not work out* (Mrs Gann).

'Inspection of launderette after the opening by Mrs Duncan Sandys, 30 April 1955 opening Ludwick Launderette. The equipment consists of 3 Electrolux gas-heated. electrically operated washing machines, one hydo-extractor and 6 gas-heated drying cabinets' (*CNT 75/20/MT/1202*). Mrs Sandys is seen here with her husband, the then Minister of Housing and Local Government, and (left) R.G. Gosling, Chairman of WGCDC, 1948–58.

'Beehive Lane, April 1955' (*CNT A/MT/1086*). *The Beehive was way out in the sticks!* Beehive Lane was *where you played tennis . . . and then called in at the Beehive afterwards, now a Beefeater* (Rosemary Mitchell); and it was *where you walked on a Sunday with the pram. It was out in the country* (Derek Greener). Nearby Beehive Green was based on the original gardens of Ludwick Corner, family home and headquarters of Frank Murphy's pioneering new company of the late 1930s: 'I've decided to cross the railway to join my workers!' Following the collapse of the company in 1940, his wife Hilda ran a guest house there for two years – for new ICI staff and visiting film stars and directors. Called locally Maggie Murphy's, it was later converted into flats.

'Cole Green Lane, rented WHDC housing 1970' (*CNT S/2113/11*). The Chieftain pub on the right of the picture was once called 'The Woodman of Bottom Hyde'. *When we came, the old city finished at The Woodman. . . . There just weren't the houses then. Just past the Woodman, there was a big number of prefabs, then (1949) they started building the big estates* (Anne Hazelwood). By 1954 the new three-storey houses were described as 'unusual looking homes'. But there were snags: the weekly rent of 46s 2d; the heating (one woman complained she had to have the boiler on for four hours without getting the water hot); the concrete-like gardens which needed a bulldozer on them; and the extra flight – 'a little tiring when you have to go up and down to the children' (*WT*).

'Aerial of Homestead, 18.8.51' (*CNT B26/5963/B*). Salisbury Road crosses the top; Homestead is centre left with Marley Road meeting Cole Green bottom right. Shortlands Green is top right. *I was born at home in Shortlands Green. It was winter-time, January 1942. My aunt came over to look after me. It was bitterly cold. My dad hadn't got any coal and she sent him out to look for some – where was he going to look for coal in the middle of winter with a war on? During the war, I can remember a lot of men in uniform coming to the house. I think it was my mum's brother turned up driving this big army lorry. They all came into my mum's house - there was always tea on the go. I was told to take a cup of tea out to the prisoner. I thought it was a German but later I learned it was one of their own who'd escaped. PoWs built a lot of the prefabs which have gone. I remember a girl older than me taking me for a walk. We went from Shortlands Green, over to the back of the allotments, walked through to Cole Green Lane – she said she wanted to watch the prefabs being built. I know now that it was because the Italian prisoners of war were there* (Joan Lammiman). *There were a lot of*

*Italian prisoners from Hemel Hempstead. They used to come by a little green van. It was run by the War Committee, bringing these prisoners into the Garden City to be allocated to different farms in the area. They used to pick me up with these prisoners, so I learnt a bit of Italian! Some of them married English people, you know. They seemed happy enough. Italians are a happy breed of people, aren't they?* (Charlie Green).

'Homestead Court Hotel, *c.* 1950' (*CNT B/27/15833/4*). Homestead Lane used to be known as School Lane and saw WHDC's first housing scheme in 1949. New flats in Homestead Court were first occupied in 1950. The hotel itself was bought by Cresta in 1980, acquired from Granada Forte in May 1996 by Regal, which was itself taken over by Corus in 1999. *In 1951 we lived in the flats which surrounded the hotel. I worked for the Development Corporation at that time, and I was invited to a cocktail party for its opening. Being young and very stupid, I didn't realise that you didn't drink and not eat, and I remember staggering across the verge back to the flat – feeling very sick!* (Rosemary Mitchell).

'UDC housing in Leigh Common showing open treatment, July 1955' (*CNT A/MT/1563*). Looking towards Homestead Lane, the King George Playing fields can be seen beyond. In 1946 nearby Hunters Way had the first five permanent houses completed since the war: 'One of the lucky five is Napoleon (see p. 103) aged 22, youngest of five sailor sons of Mr and Mrs William Potter of 14 Applecroft Road who have lived there since 1923. Their 18 grandchildren and 1 great-grandchild are all in WGC. . . .' (*WT*).

Same view, 1999 (*MH*). The 'open treatment' has been filled somewhat by trees, garden hedges and cars. The first meeting of United Reformed Church took place in 1923 in the Hatfield Hyde village club-room, where nearby Four Acres now is, facing on to Hollybush Lane. *It was an unforgettable experience, a soaking wet stormy night and blowing a gale. Inside the little room with a roaring fire in the corner were gathered some 60 villagers, nearly all the population!* (Edmond Barraclough).

'Hatfield Hyde Cricket Club Old Time Cricket Match, *c. 1950*' (*CNT 73/18*). The cricket club started in 1889 with Mr J.H. Ivory as the first Honorary Secretary and its first playing pitch in 'Charity' fields near Ludwick Corner; later the club played in part of the grounds of Homestead Court. More open-air entertainment was provided by the Salvation Army playing and singing on Hatfield Hyde village green. Each house would lend a couple of chairs for people to sit on.

'Children's Play Space, King George V Playing Fields, 1964' (*CNT KW838/25*). The area was conveyed to the Urban District Council (UDC) from the WGCC in 1936 for open space. It was used for football, hockey and bowls; the sports pavilion opened in 1968. Among children's playground games recalled in the early years of the Garden City are conkers, hopscotch and *'bussing up': two children stood shoulder to shoulder and joined hands behind their backs; a third child behind guided them with a loop of rope or string around their shoulders, in imitation of a horse-drawn bus as they trotted round the playground* (Alec Scott).

'Aerial of the South East area – Woodhall, June 1962' (*CNT M/25012/A*). Cole Green Lane crosses the picture, bottom to top, passing on its right Upperfield with Cowper Road, Ludwick Way and Woodhall Parade (with Holwell Road crossing the top right corner) and Gooseacre top left. In 1926 a local reporter visited 'The Tunnellers' near the top of Ludwick Way, creating a link with the mains sewage system. He found them 28 ft down working with picks by candlelight 'in a crouching position . . . hot and tired and dirty, breathing bad air, stripped almost to the waist, hacking their way through . . . in order to provide drainage and sanitation for houses [existing] so far only on paper, but which will soon be pleasant little family homes along the sides of the new road' (*WGCT*). The Woodhall branch of Welwyn Stores opened in 1938, the first example of a planned shopping arcade anywhere in the country. The first ever self-service store (Co-op) opened in 1950. *There was a big Fine Fare shop selling lots of odds and ends. I used to get a threepenny bag of broken biscuits for the children which came in very handy* (Mrs Gann). *It had an 'In and Out' shop where we could use our BU's points left over from the (wartime) rationing system* (Mrs Abbott). *You'd walk every week to the Health Centre to have the babies weighed . . . get your Ostermilk and your orange juice, then the children went to the dentist there* (Anne Hazelwood).

'Woodhall shops, showing enlarged parking area, 1969' (*CNT R/1920/5*)'. Originally a stud farm was said to have existed on the site with paddocks and loose boxes for brood mares and offspring. From the shopping centre to Heronswood was *the racecourse, a training ground for farmers' point-to-point, later used for training mules and horses and men for service during the First World War. Columns could be seen along the narrow lanes, horses and mules harnessed to and drawing the gun limbers. Others would be led or ridden along, or cantered across the meadows all in readiness for more serious action overseas* (C.V. Ivory). In 1962 Hilda Golder shot and killed her violent husband one breakfast time in their house in Cole Green Lane (leading off from the bottom of the picture). Twenty years before, another Hilda, of nearby Ludwick Corner, had also had a troubled marriage. In 1942, Hilda Murphy, District Commissioner of Guides, divorced her famous entrepreneur husband, Frank. After the sudden death of their son from a rare reaction to a smallpox vaccination, Frank had set up home with their daughter-in-law Audrey. *Frank had a brilliant mind, a lovely sense of humour and a loving heart. He was a lonely man who with the coming years would become ever more lonely. He was in love with me in 1942 and I loved him* (Audrey Murphy). They married in Canada in 1947, but *it all fell apart in a young country with young people and the 26-year gap became overwhelming* (ibid).

'Aerial of Broadwater Road factories 26.6.1957' (*CNT C/16.943/B*). Peartree Lane crosses the picture from the left, just above Ludwick Way, and meets Tewin Road (centre), with Swallowfields beneath; the railway runs across the top third of the picture; Bridge Road East crosses it top right, and continues diagonally into Heronswood bottom left. *In Heronswood the roads were unfinished but I was thrilled to see the house allocated to us (via the Post Office), that it seemed to have a lot of glass, and to have a side entrance was a big bonus. What was best was having a place of our own having lived with my parents since getting married. The rent was £2.2s. We had the chance to start a new life but still quite close to London to visit our parents quite easily. Bus services were almost non-existent, however* (Mr and Mrs Abbott).

Frank Murphy's first factory was near the top of Broadwater Road, opposite Shredded Wheat (top right). The stories about him and his house at Ludwick Corner abound: the original house had been built in about 1910 by Lord Salisbury, allegedly to house his paramour Mrs Tweedie and her children. Unusually for the 1930s, when Frank and Hilda Murphy moved in, it had central heating. It also had 20 ft square rooms, an extensive garden and an adjacent spinney. Frank Murphy applied for planning permission in 1940 to develop this spinney for the new company he had set up in the house, arguing that existing factory sites were too ugly. He lost on appeal, possibly because he had criticised publicly the fact that WGC planners had given workers' housing on the east side a far less pleasant environment than the middle-class commuters on the west.

*Frank Murphy was an interesting man. I had to plough up his garden once. He lived in that big house in Cole Green Lane – it was pulled down eventually and built on. . . . Peartree School had enormous playing fields at the back, and all these council houses backed on to them and everyone threw their rubbish over. Also buried were these narrow gauge railway lines. [During the war] I was told to plough this up – it was mostly old iron. I had a tractor and a trailer with a 500 gallon tank on board . . . and behind that I pulled a plough. Frank Murphy's garden wasn't very big, about half an acre, but everywhere where there was bare land had to be ploughed up. I was busy ploughing this large lawn, when suddenly the tractor started to sink – there was an underground stream. I sank right up to the axles and beyond, so I went and phoned up the 'War Ag' as it was called and told them what had happened, and they said they'd send another tractor along to pull me out. I said, No, a tractor won't pull me out, I'm sunk right in! And they had to get heavy lifting tackle to get me out* (Ralph Parkes-Pfeil).

'UDC Housing in Salisbury Road showing tree planting, July 1955' (*CNT A/MT/1555*). In 1934 a 17-year old resident, in charge of heating the boilers at the Broadwater Road Feddon & Bond factory, attempted 'to revive a dull fire with some oil. . . . He became a mass of flames from head to foot'. A neighbour and work-mate, Tom Spalding, quickly threw water over him. Later, 'by good fortune . . . the quantities of lubricating oil [available] were applied to his burns' (*WT*). Behind the houses, *a little Cabin shop sold everything for kids: a cone of sweets, dolly mixtures. My gran and granddad always used to give me a halfpenny, to wait for the Walls man at the end of the road. He came on his bike, and you'd get snowfruit, which was a lolly really* (Anne Hazelwood).

Joan Beck aged 15 in Cowper Road, just off Cole Green Road, looking into Upperfield (*courtesy Joan Lammiman, née Beck*). This was in 1956, ten years after the family moved there from Shortlands Green. *I remember that move – Dad loading up the lorry, moving in during November time. It was bitterly cold, and (again) we had no coal to light a fire with. . . . It was a much bigger house. My sister was only 18 months old. They were trying to make the beds up at night time – it was all new to us. My brother came along in 1950. That was it then. . . . When it was cold, my mum used to give me a hot water bottle to hold. My mum's family would come down from the north to visit because where they were living, the conditions weren't that great. This to them was luxury – indoor toilets! It used to fascinate me to go up north because my granny used to have a yard with a toilet there – she used to do all her washing out in the back yard* (Joan Lammiman).

Mrs Edith Beck in the back garden of her house in Ethelred Close, 1940 (*courtesy Joan Lammiman*). The Beck family is one of three featured here which characterise the experiences for residents from the 1940s to the 1980s when many of the original houses built for workers were demolished and replaced. Joan Lammiman, Edith Beck's eldest daughter, recalls: *My parents came from the north of England. My dad was sent down here, to Croydon at first, to work. He moved to Hatfield and my grandfather brought all his family down (including) several brothers. They all lived in Hatfield apart from my dad and sister. My mum came down from the north, they married and they got a house in Ethelred Close. . . . They were married in '38, and it wasn't long after that that they got it. I think my mum was sad that the first house she ever lived in here was knocked down. The landscape seems to have changed up there. They pulled them down in 1983.*

The same view in 1983, when Joan Lammiman visited her parents' first WGC home, in Ethelred Close, shortly before its demolition (*Tony Lammiman*).

Mrs Emily Hazelwood, Ted Hazelwood's mother, outside 18 Ethelred Close, 19 January 1948 (*courtesy Ted Hazelwood*). The second family, the Hazelwoods, were neighbours to the third, the Wards. Anne Hazelwood (née Ward) recalls: *I came in September '39. My dad was a Grenadier Guard. We were at Wellington Barracks. War broke out in '39 and threw all the families out. My father had relatives here. My maiden name was Ward – Irish of course. My father's relatives found us a house, in Ethelred Close. . . . It was half wooden clad, three bedrooms, had a bathroom, kitchen and one living room. I was seven. I'd always lived in barracks. It made a big difference for me. Ted lived in the same close – he lived at 18 and I lived at no. 3. It was a nice little community, Ethelred Close. We'd got quite a lot of mums without dads there – they were away in the war. [There were] a lot of children. I think cul-de-sacs become little communities.*

Anne Ward and Ted Hazelwood played together as children: *We played in the streets. As kids, we played round the lamp-posts. [We'd play] skipping – across the road with the clothesline* (Anne). *'Canon' was three sticks like a wicket that you stood up against a lamp-post or gatepost, and threw the ball at it. Then, when they went down, one team had to run and hide. The idea was that the team that finds you had to build this wicket back up again, without being hit by the other team with the ball* (Ted).

Ted Hazelwood with his father in 1951 at the junction of Ludwick way and Longlands Road (*Ted Hazelwood*). Ted recalls: *My father's house was bigger than others,because we had the extra bit over the alleyway. The front bedroom took up the whole width of the house. It was a very large room. So they could have made those into a bathroom and a bedroom and still end up with a bigger bedroom than you get nowadays.* However, when Ted and Anne married in 1953, there were no new houses available, and they had to move in with Ted's parents and his brother and sister-in-law — all living at no. 18. *We were lucky that the Development Corporation started up!.. After we'd left his dad's house, they did go and do up [all the concrete houses]. They put a proper bathroom in upstairs, extended the kitchen, and in these houses where they had the bath in the kitchen, they put an outside bathroom that sort of came in to the house. So they did a lot of renovation* (Anne).

Joan Beck's Great Grandma May, Granny Young, and Aunt Molly in Ethelred Close, *c.* 1940 (*courtesy Joan Lammiman, née Beck*). Wartime for Ethelred residents, especially the children, provided some vivid experiences: Ted and Anne Hazelwood recall: *There was a big field next to Ethelred Close – a bomb fell right in the middle of it! It was most exciting, it wasn't frightening really. The explosion shook the house. You'd hear the whistles then the thumps, but once it's down, it's down, though not on you. . . . We used to walk from Ethelred Close to school every morning. I remember the playground, just on the edge of the field, they built some shelters, with no windows because the school was all windows. Every time the sirens went we all had to dash over...We used to sleep on the floor downstairs,bring the bedding downstairs during the war, the old eiderdown and blanket. You'd wait for the All-Clear, because if it was past twelve o'clock, you didn't have to go to school. You'd say, Ah! It's ten past twelve, the All-Clear's gone – we don't have to go to school, Mum. She'd say, Oh yes you do!*

*Towards the end of the war we got the buzz-bombs. If there was a siren during the school day, we used to have to take something over there to amuse ourselves – I used to do yards of french knitting to pass the time* (Anne Hazelwood).

Edith Beck (Joan Lammiman's mother) and her sister Mollie with Trixie the dog, *c.* 1940 (*courtesy Joan Lammiman*). Young women were billeted on Ethelred residents during the war. Anne Hazelwood recalls: *We had the Norton's Bluebells. They* (Norton's Grinding Wheels factory) *had girls from up north to work there. They were called the Norton's Bluebells because they wore blue overalls. I remember Doris . . . they were northern girls, spoke funny to us. Some came from Norfolk. They spoke even funnier. You didn't get about much in those days. Their accent was much more pronounced.*

'Street in Peartree celebrates with a sit-down tea, 1945' (*From WGC residents' handbook 1946, courtesy Joan Lammiman*). *At the end of the war, at the VJ party in Ethelred Close, we had tables down the middle of the close* (Anne Hazelwood). *The wonderful thing with parties is that my dad used to play the piano – and he was self-taught* (Ted Hazelwood).

'Victory revels: Flashlight picture of crowds dancing in Peartree Streets 1945' (*From WGC residents' handbook 1946, courtesy Joan Lammiman*). *You had your little bits of glory. Mr Gardener (a neighbour in Ethelred Close) used to drive a Rolls-Royce – he was a chauffeur for some big family and he occasionally drove his Rolls-Royce home. I remember at the end of the war, we had a big bonfire in the middle of the road, and he came out with this magic fluid and threw it on the bonfire and Whoosh! 'Course, it was a little drop of petrol that he'd had* (Ted Hazelwood).

The Peartree School (*WGC citizens' handbook, 1930, courtesy Ann Adams*). This famous picture belies the trauma experienced by some children when they were transferred at 11 from Peartree to Handside School on the 'other side': *It was entry to an alien world far from home . . . a world peopled by unfriendly strangers who we neither understood nor liked. . . . We left the hopes of our parents and envy of our friends to meet only disdain and dismissal for our unacceptable factory-land background. Despite the smart uniforms and satchels, we were at once picked out for what we were – intruders infiltrating a cosy club which never expected to embrace those from across the tracks. The stigma long remained, in some for ever* (David Smith, quoted by de Soissons).

Ludwick School staff, 1939 (*courtesy Joan Lammiman*). This infants' school opened in 1932 in Holwell Road and subsequently became Holwell School. It catered for children from 5 to 7 after which they were transferred to Peartree. *The thing I hated about the school was that it had outside toilets. In the winter time, it used to freeze up. You had to queue up to go to what toilets they had indoors* (Joan Lammiman). Miss Smith [back row, second from right] was a teacher at the school between 1937 and 1951. She recorded her time there with many photographs and *kept a log of all the children's names, when they were born, where they lived, including 17 evacuees [during the war]. I started there in 1948* (ibid).

The Ludwick School teachers listed by Miss Smith on this photograph are Misses Bush, Roth, Gilmore, Salmon, Sawfield, Collins, McKelvie, Johnson and Bradshaw, July 1950 (*courtesy Joan Lammiman née Beck*). Joan Beck's later school experiences were at Oaken Grove. *I went to the Howard School (later called St John Newsome). It was the first school to be built this side of the town after the war. It opened in 1953. My age group was the first intake at 11. I enjoyed it, [but] there were some rough teachers. Mr Sargerson was horrible, a bully. He must have come out of the army. . . . He taught Maths. I hated Maths. He was our form teacher as well, for two years. The school closed down in September 1998, 'surplus to requirements'.*

Miss Smith, *c.* 1950 (*courtesy Joan Lammiman*). *Miss Smith had a flat here, round the corner and she did an exchange in South Africa. I remember her telling me she came from Nottingham. She turned up late one evening with her bike and she had lodgings way out in a farm cottage with a family, on the old Panshanger estate – she had to ride to school in all weathers. She started about 1937–8 and stayed until the early '50s* (Joan Lammiman). Joan befriended her again in the 1980s when Miss Smith was living alone among all her school memorabilia. She died in 1985.

The Ludwick School Lorry, 1949 (*Miss Smith, courtesy Joan Lammiman*). *I remember that lorry being on the playground. It was just dumped there and we played on it* (Joan Lammiman).

The Ludwick School Garden, 1949 (*Miss Smith, courtesy Joan Lammiman*). In the 1930s there was a campaign for a free Nursery School in Peartree, with a survey of 1000 houses, 30% of which had children of nursery age. Most of these families had only 60% of the recommended norm to spend on food; and the birth rate in Peartree was 30% higher than in the rest of Herts. 'Figures were also given showing the numbers of cases of defective teeth, tonsils, posture and certified malnutrition in the children entering Ludwick School. . . . Much of this could be wiped out and much more considerably lessened by the proper diet, environment and regular medical inspection provided in a Nursery School' (*WT*). A small nursery school was subsequently built.

'Opening of Peartree Girls' Club by Mr R.L. Reiss, 1951, in premises previously occupied by the Methodist Church' (*CNT 73/18/10*). Richard Reiss was a Director of the original WGCC and Vice-Chairman of WHDC 1948–52. Described by Fred Osborn as 'a man of sincere devotion to public welfare and political force', he was also instrumental in developing the Peartree Boys' Club. In December 1935 the *Welwyn Times* announced its opening with: 'Bridging the railway line: The new Peartree Boys club is to cater first for working boys who have recently left school . . . a ballet was put on by "London Working lads" of Tonbridge and Cheltenham Missions.'

'Peartree Girls' Club Sewing Class, May 1955' (*CNT 75/24/MC/0024*). During the war the Boys' Club became the Peartree Maternity Hospital. *[I had] my second baby there. They didn't get me into the delivery ward quick enough, so I had to have it in the main ward. Sister Judge and Sister Duke were in charge. They were as chalk and cheese, Sister Duke being very gentle, while Sister Judge was more like a sergeant major but she was not less kind and caring. In those days, one had to stay in hospital for at least a week after giving birth* (Helga Lomas). *Our eldest daughter was born there in 1953. Brian wasn't allowed to wait and had to walk back to Homestead Court carrying all my clothes in a bundle* (Rosemary Mitchell).

'Peartree Girls' Club Ballroom Dancing, May 1955' (*CNT 75/24/MC/00211*). The Boys' Club had more vigorous pursuits. In January 1946 'spectators had an unexpected treat at the end of the Boxing Display. . . . During an exhibition fight between two heavy lads, one of the contestants was knocked through the ropes and the stage collapsed' (*WT*). Betty Scales recalls: *We came in '26. My mother was expecting my brother 6 weeks later and the taxi put her off at Peartree where the Boys' Club is now and they had to walk from there to Mill Green because the road was unmade.*

'Opening of YMCA Residential Club, Peartree Lane, 1.7.67, the first of its kind in Britain co-operatively sponsored by local employees, the first with accommodation for young women. Shown is one of nine bedrooms for them; there are 71 rooms for youths' (*CNT 75/11/190667 YM4-5*).

'Peartree Close, 12.11.65: The Hatfield Hyde WI present 12 Golden Jubilee trees to commemorate their Golden Jubilee. Founder members Miss Jessie Bracey and Mrs Agnes Cochrane are seen placing the plaque in position' (*CNT 74/6/19*). Derek Greener remembers: *We had a 90-ft garden in Peartree Close. There's now three houses on that garden.*

'OAP flats Peartree Close, July 1966' (*CNT P/1331/15*). The 18th-century Peartree Farm was sited nearby. In the early 19th century a mole-catcher, Thomas Ensom, kept a beerhouse there. The farm consisted originally of 200 acres with a farmhouse where the shops are now and had orchards and peacocks. It was owned by Lord Salisbury, and farmed by a Scot, James Hunter, who reportedly resented the Garden City settlers, became a recluse, and died in 1938. *Mr and Mrs Hunter often gave prizes at the church fetes and judged the events* ('RT').

Peartree Lane, *c.* 1980 (*Tony Lammiman*). The first brick was laid in 1925. By September 1934 all the houses were full. *Peartree Lane was our first house, when Peartree really had a village atmosphere* (Derek and Dorothy Greener). In 1930, further down the road, a new fish restaurant opened, declaring 'All expectations will be surpassed. All the smell which in old days used to make a "fried fish shop" rather objectionable to some critical people is in these days consumed in the fire of the range itself. [Its] deep pans of boiling oil instantly cover the fish sealing every atom of goodness within the crisp gold batter.' A month later, 43 residents signed a protest: 'The offensive smell is continuous and objectionable. [We deplore] the noise and bad language of a certain crowd of youths' (*WT*).

Peartree Lane, 1983 (*Tony Lammiman*). *It was winter time, and we went out for a walk to take pictures of the houses that were being pulled down. . . . I was sad to see them go because although they were very old, and needed a lot of money spent on them, I just feel they've taken the character of the town away, because nobody would know now that they were there. Peartree Lane, Broadwater Road, Woodhall Court, Peartree Court, Holwell Road – they've kept the names but the houses have all gone. They were built as experimental houses and weren't meant to last longer than 20 years, but they just kept going. They were very good houses, quite roomy* (Joan Lammiman).

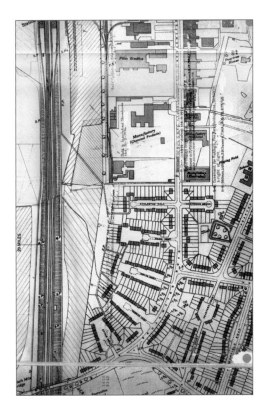

Map of Broadwater Road area showing housing layout from about 1935 (*Railtrack Property*). Some of the original estates – now demolished – can be seen around Peartree Lane, Broadwater Road, Woodhall Court, Peartree Court, Holwell Road and Woodhall Lane as well as some of the first Broadwater Road factories.

Ted Hazelwood with his father, two cousins visiting from London, and Alan Sugg in Peartree Lane, 1951 (*courtesy Ted Hazelwood*).

John Hazelwood (second from right) at a wartime St George's Day ceremony in Peartree Lane, 1944 (*courtesy Ted Hazelwood*). *My brother was at this scouts' do in the Peartree Car Park near Peartree Stores.* One Peartree Lane firm, British Lead Mills Ltd, was fined £2 with 6*d* costs for showing 'very bright lights from four skylights' during the blackout. So many cases were being reported that the Chairman of the Welwyn sessions said: 'The penalty for these offences is £100. We are letting people off lightly, yet more and more are coming.' He subsequently fined Dawnays £10 with 7*d* costs (*WT*, 1940).

Ted Hazelwood (front row, fifth from right) in the line-up to meet Princess Marina, the Duchess of Kent, 1941 (*courtesy Ted Hazelwood*). *I can just remember this sort of famous person in front of me. She didn't speak to me. . . .*

The junction of Holwell Road with Peartree Lane, *c.* 1980 (*Tony Lammiman*). The grassy area at this south-west end of Peartree Lane reportedly marks a medieval homestead site, at least 600 years old. Residents of the area in 1934 saw 'some excitement . . . in Holwell Road on Whit Monday when at about 5.45 in the afternoon, a Hitchin-bound bus caught fire by the back wheels due to the friction of the brake linings. While the conductor rescued the precious tickets from the "burning deck", the driver and others rushed inside one of the houses for buckets of water and a call was put through to the Brigade. Damage was estimated at about £10. . . .' (*WT*).

Holwell Road houses being demolished, 1983 (*Tony Lammiman*). *Holwell Road was quite a nice road. We lived at the top, but they pulled the houses down and built six more in their place. We had long gardens and there was a spinney at the back where we used to go to play. There was a swing and see-saw, so that mother could call over from the kitchen door, 'Dinner's ready!' so we weren't too far away. I'd walk from there to the Convent School in Parkway and back - and for dinner - four times a day* (Dorothea Bagge). *I used to take my son to Holwell Road School which was a 'Free Expression' School. It was quite a long walk from our house in Heronswood along Cole Green Lane and up to Woodhall and past!* (Mrs Abbott).

Woodhall Court shortly before demolition, 1983 (*Tony Lammiman*).

The top of Woodhall Lane, shortly before demolition, 1983 (*Tony Lammiman*). Originally this was the site of an ancient manor belonging to the Bassingbourne family (from 1198) which passed to the Botelers then the Shallcrosses. It later became Woodhall Lodge Farm, specialising in pig farming and managed by Mr Henson. Woodhall Farm was also owned by Lord Salisbury and farmed by the Peart family who ran a herd of pedigree Friesians; this was taken over by the Agricultural Guild in 1920. The Flint Cottage (see p. 10) was half-way up Woodhall Lane.

Woodhall Court and Peartree Court, *c.* 1930 (*courtesy Ann Adams*). The original caption, 'A charming example of the open front garden', comes from the 1930 handbook whose preface states: 'A whole town can be beautiful. That is one of the things WGC has been built to prove. This book is published 10 years after the first brick was laid. The photographs, taken in 1929 and 1930, give some idea of the success attained. Beauty in the town, as these pictures plainly show, depends upon the design and arrangement of groups of houses and of entire streets, not upon the architecture of individual houses alone. The creation, by good design and skilful planting, of harmonious and interesting street effects, is an art in which WGC has led the world.'

Woodhall Court being demolished, 1983 (*Tony Lammiman*). This photograph coincidentally captured the last hours of the same houses over fifty years later, the shot being taken further back.

'Creswick Court, 1976' (*CNT S/3652/25*). These workers' houses, just of the southern end of Broadwater Road, were demolished in 1980. *They've pulled all the concrete houses down now. Condensation was bad – the wallpaper used to peel off* (Walter Broughton).

'Moss Green, 1961' (*CNT L/JC/DC/120*). Residents in this development just off the western end of Woodhall Lane, practically unchanged in 40 years, saw all around it disappear.

Holwell Road and Broadwater Road, *c.* 1930 (*courtesy Ann Adams*). The caption reads 'Near the Moat Wood and Goblins Green'. Around this area and nearby Broadwater Crescent the WGCC built 450 concrete houses for local employees, but following 'serious maintenance problems' they too were demolished in the 1980s.

'Sectional factories, Broadwater Road, 1962' (*CNT K/L259/IIA*). This is a more familiar view of the road. These small factories also had problems. In 1937 a 14-year-old boy of Salisbury Gardens, having just started work at Unity Heating, tried to replace a belt which kept coming off a hacksaw machine, used for cutting iron bars. 'He was lifted from the floor by the belting and carried up to the shafting. His arm was wrapped round the shaft and broken in three places. It was not usual in the works to stop the shafting to replace belts.' The Chairman and Managing Director said he took 'a deep interest in his works and the welfare of his employees. He had never seen a guard on that type of hacksaw.' The company was fined £5 for failing to fence machinery with 5s costs (*WT*).

Anna Neagle as Florence Nightingale, filming for *The Lady with the Lamp* with local residents Ted Hazelwood, fireman (left) and Harry Page, driver, 1951 (*courtesy Ted Hazelwood*). 'The actual shots . . . were to show the Station Master and his assistant discussing the home-coming of Florence Nightingale when she surprises them by arriving, unheralded, at the station. . . . Twice there were pauses to wait for an aeroplane to pass out of earshot, and another while Miss Neagle had her hair rearranged' (*WT*). Ted Hazelwood remembers: *We practised all Sunday and filmed all Monday; when we saw the film, you just saw the top of (my) hat go by. The whole scene lasted 20 seconds! We did very well out of it actually: we got paid by the railway, and the film company, and we got food!* The Garden City was a strong attraction for the film industry. The British Instructional Film Co., 'Hertfordshire's Hollywood', occupied the arched-roof building in Broadwater Road, an original part of the studio (currently used by Polycell). Over 80 films were made there between 1932 and 1942; it closed in 1952. Many residents recall it: Sonja Pooley's husband looked after the horses there as a schoolboy, as did Stan Scales: *I held the horses for the actors. I used to dash in from school. They'd give us a sandwich at lunchtime – it was lovely!* Anne Hazelwood remembers her uncle *used to go and paint the scenery there . . . we used to go and watch if anything was being filmed.* Alec Scott has a unique reminiscence, which deserves to be quoted in full: *Together with my brother Tom, I was in the 1st WGC Scout Troop from about 1933 to 1936. It was this circumstance that gave rise to my very brief career in films. In 1935 the Silver Jubilee of King George V was celebrated. A commemorative film was made, largely at the Film Studios in Broadwater Road. One day Captain Kelly knocked at our door to tell us that the film company needed a pair of scouts for a short scene and asked if we would like to go along. Willing to try anything, we donned our uniforms and went down to the Studios. It appeared that they were depicting life on the home front in WW1 when Boy Scouts used bugles for sounding air-raid alarms and the 'All Clear' afterwards. Neither Tom nor I had ever touched a bugle, let alone blown one, a fact which seemed to surprise the film people. Nevertheless, they hauled one out from somewhere, gave me a rough idea of the two notes necessary for the 'All Clear', and a soundproof cupboard for a while so I could practise. When I had achieved an approximation of the sounds required, they let me out. We were plastered with yellowish make-up and work on the 'tedious brief scene' began. Tom stood beside me as I blew. The camera crew winced visibly. Tom then had to utter some suitably fearless words and the scene was over. I was told not to worry about my appalling bugle notes; they would dub in something more authentic. We were paid half a guinea each, the first money we had ever earned. The yellow make-up lingered on the outskirts of our faces for a day or two and drew remarks at school.*

'Industry at Welwyn, 1938: Cresta Silks' (*CNT 76/17*). Althea Richardson remembers going to the workroom as a little girl when her step-father, Langdon-Davies, worked for the owner, Tom Heron (father to the acclaimed artist, Patrick). *They were working with fabulous materials, the finest silk. I remember Langdon saying, Tom Heron could pick up a piece of silk, rub it through his fingers and feel the quality and what sort of worm it came from. The designs were by some very well-known artists, wonderful designs. I was allowed to choose the scraps. They had tea-chests, and they'd put the scraps in as the women worked on the dresses. . . . They said, Choose materials for your dolls' clothes, so I had fabulously dressed dolls in these lovely materials.*

'Industry at Welwyn, 1938: Sweets Candy Company' (*CNT 76/17*). *If you worked in the sweet factory, you could eat as many sweets as you liked for the first week. After that, you never touched them* (Mrs Dalhousie-Young).

'Industry at Welwyn, 1938: Shredded Wheat' (*CNT 76/17*). Welgar (from WELyn GARden), was bought by Nabisco in 1928. In 1924 work was begun on the factory: 'many of the features of the company's famous factory at Niagara are to be repeated. There is no suggestion, however that either of our local rivers, the Lea or the Mimram, will (like Niagara Falls) provide the power for driving the wonderful machinery employed in turning our shredded wheat. . . . A palace of crystal, its great walls (are) held together by slender white tiled columns of concrete' (*WT*). It opened in 1925 with 100 workers, most of them women; by 1986 there were 1,000. *The early morning smell of the Shredded Wheat biscuits as they were being cooked – wonderful!* (Rosemary Mitchell).

'WGC New Town (Area no. 2), Hatfield Hyde Areas 2 & 3, 5.9.53' (*CNT A/11108/B*). The white Shredded Wheat factory is top centre with the railway running diagonally behind it and Broadwater Road before. St Mary Magdalene Church is almost dead centre with King George Playing fields to the right. The still-eponymous Hollybush Lane emerges bottom left, crossing the newly carved developments of Howlands, Mountway and Golden Dell (foreground).

'Opening by Mr and Mrs Duncan Sandys of 35 Golden Dell for Mr and Mrs Edkins, 30.4.1955' (*CNT 75/20/MT/00222*). This was considered to be 'a typical small 3-bedroom (4 persons') house', costing £1,446, or £1 6s rent per week.

'Pinnate Place Play area 1969' (*CNT R/1920/4*).

'The Hollybush and houses in Howlands and Pinnate Place, 1959' (*CNT G/CW/10358*). The Hollybush was the first post-war pub to open, in 1958, for the Hollybush and Howlands area of Hatfield Hyde.

'Aerial of Hatfield Hyde showing Boundary Lane (left), Middlefield, Lady Grove and Linkfields (centre), Howlands (centre right), Walnut Grove (right) and site for shops and pub (bottom)' (*CNT C/16.952/B*). The eastern side of the Garden City from the railway to the hamlet of Hatfield Hyde had been farmland, largely cornfields. *We lived in Boundary Lane. . . . It was in December 1956 that my husband, who had been appointed to the estates department of the Development Corporation, brought me to pick up the keys to our first house . . . situated near the edge of the town. No sooner had we settled in than we acquired bikes* (Helga Lomas).

# CHAPTER TWO

# PANSHANGER & THE NORTH-EAST

Mr and Mrs Walter Broughton meet the Queen Mother at the opening of Elizabeth House, Moors Walk, Panshanger in November 1983 *(courtesy Walter Broughton)*. *We were the first residents here in 1983 when it was opened by the Queen Mother. She was in this room. She's a very nice old lady – no side, no cut-glass accent or anything like that. It was just pleasant to talk to her. We got on very well. She stopped in here which was quite a lot of the time. I told her I was a Hertfordshire Hedgehog. She said, What do you mean? Well, I said, people in Yorkshire are known as tykes, in Newcastle they're Geordies, but in Hertfordshire, they're Hedgehogs! I used to run the Social Club here – bingo, whist drives, parties, outings to Woburn and Whipsnade, all sorts of things. We'd always got something on. (Walter Broughton).*

Panshanger was named reputedly from 'Paine's hangre' – a wooded slope. Indeed, two saw mills were especially erected to process the wood cut by prisoners of war from the Panshanger camp – although the oaks they felled came from Sherrards Wood in the west. In the First World War German prisoners were brought in by cart to cut down trees to be used as sleepers for the forward lines in Flanders and France; in the Second World War prisoners of war were again housed at Panshanger to cut the wood for timber. Notwithstanding, the noted Panshanger Oak in Panshanger Park was said in 1962 to be the oldest in England. *If you got as far as Panshanger there was nightingales* (Derek Greener).

Apart from a few scattered hamlets and farms – the long-settled Grub's Barn and Hern Farm for example – and a dummy airfield to deceive German bombers, the north-east part of the Garden City was *an empty quarter: as scouts we sometimes played 'wide games' in the fields, but there was little else to attract us – except for the long downhill stretch of the light railway to the gravel pit at Digswell. The line ran from the engine shed where Campus West now stands, up Digswell Road, over the main railway at Singlers Bridge and then there was the straight run down to the pit. It was a great day when we could find a truck to 'borrow' for the exhilarating ride. Returning the truck? We never gave it a thought. I'm afraid I look back now with some disapproval on my younger self* (Alec Scott).

When the WGCDC took over from the WGCC in 1948 the south-west quarter of the Garden City was already 'largely completed'. In its handbook of 1963 WGCDC stated that the south-east was currently the centre of DC activity; that the north-west was soon to be developed, and the north-east was to be left for 'natural increase'. However, large-scale development in the sector started in 1964: 'a few old cottages and an old

barn surrounded by fields became the largest housing development in the area' (Filler). The modern open-plan design was much criticised for being 'anti-garden city' with its much higher densities: *They built Panshanger, but to me it doesn't resemble the Garden City – I call it West Hertford* (Ralph Parkes-Pfeil). Many of the more picturesque names of the area (from the 1841 Tithe Apportionment map) finally disappeared: Gutteridge Grove Field, Fishpond Field, Calves Pightle, Cob Lane Field, Hitches, Carthorse Field, Hither Round Field, Green Sauce Field, Middle Mead.

'Mr and Mrs W.J. Hill of 22 Windhill, the first tenants to move into the Panshanger area, 7.4.66' (*CNT 75/11/1245/33*).

'Broomhills – Panshanger scheme no. 1. Bungalow no. 37 and houses nos 35–3. Built for and sold by CNT, February 1967' (*CNT P/1430/11*). In 1966, when the WGCDC was wound up, and the CNT took over, housing construction gathered pace. This then sparse-looking development at Broomhills was overlooked by the Smith Kline Beecham factory (left) with little evidence of the famed Garden City trees.

The same view, 1999 (*author*). 'Bungalow no. 37' can just be glimpsed through the shrubs and trees. SmithKline (*sic*) no longer dominates. The contrast in these two views, and in the pictures that follow, show how much this youngest part of the Garden City has 'come of age'.

'Panshanger 2, The Moors, 1968' (*CNT R/1779/28*). The Moors was part of a housing scheme that won a Civic Trust Award in 1968, deliberately built at low cost for young families. But the windows leaked and the brickwork was so porous that furnishings were soaked when it rained. Residents complained, too, of there being no pillar boxes, nor phone boxes, nor shops. Their local centre was not built until 10 years later.

The same view, 1999 (*author*).

'Panshanger showing new shop and sub-post office, 1969' (*CNT R/1922/17*). This little shop served the community around The Moors until the neighbourhood centre was completed in 1978.

The same view, 1999 (*author*).

'Panshanger neighbourhood centre, consisting of ground and first floor shops and community/ pastoral centre and public house, 1978' (CNT S/3897/21).

The same view, 1999 (author).

'Panshanger Hardings self-build, the first house (of 13) nearing completion, 1972' (*CNT S/2585/2*).
This would not have been possible with the original WGCC because it alone controlled the site,
design and construction of every building within the Garden City boundaries.

The same houses, 1999 (*author*). The WGCC had been at pains to explain its monopoly: 'The
division of powers and responsibilities as between the Urban Council and the WGCC is seldom
grasped by outsiders and not always understood by people who live here. Briefly the position is this.
The Urban Council, a democratically elected body, has exactly the same duties and obligations as
any Urban Council anywhere. The Company has exactly the same legal powers and responsibilities
as any landowner anywhere. The great difference [is] that the Company is the sole landowner,
[therefore] friction (between rival landowners) does not exist' (Citizens' Guide, 1946).

'Aerial of Viaduct and Nurseries, NW area, 1962: Area P completed; Area S under construction with roads and services completed on Area Q. To the left of Q are dwellings built by UDC' (*CNT M/25023/A*). This cryptic caption from WGCDC describes the Haldens and Blytheway development (top left); The Swallows and Rosedale (top centre right); the beginnings of Rowans, Flexley Wood, Swanhill, Robin Mead, Crookhams, Quick Beams, Eastor, Lumbards, Pondfield, Postfield and Sloansway (centre); and Maple Grove, Runsley and Timbercroft (centre left).

'Rosedale, with Digswell Viaduct in background, 1961 (*CNT K/JC/DC/130*). Blondin, the famous Victorian wire-walker, reputedly trained by racing across the parapets of the Digswell Viaduct.

The same view, 1999 (*author*)

'Rowans, 1968: two-bedroom bungalows and three-bedroom houses' (*CNT R/1467/15*).

The same view, 1999 (*author*).

'Darts on the Green – Eastor, NE area, 4.4.67' (*CNT P/1468/19*). The name means 'furthest east', although there are other Garden City communities that can lay claim to this now.

The same view, 1999 (*author*).

'Haldens House shops and flats, August 1964' (*CNT O/KW908/17*). In 1948 the population of this area was only 77: the Development Corporation eventually housed 12,000 here and in Panshanger. When the Mayflower pub opened in 1964 it was only the second one in the county to offer purpose-built social amenities for the whole community. The local shopping centre, shown here, opened in 1964.

The same view, 1999 (*author*).

'Haldens Adventure play space, 1967' (*CNT 74/12/1469/27*). This '60s-style playground had much in common with children's play areas earlier in the life of the Garden City – except that it was created for them, not by them. Alec Scott recalled an area in woods on the north-western side: *'Ledge Camp' was on a ledge we had dug out of the side of a swallow-hole dell. When the dell flooded the water lapped almost up the level of the 'camp' floor. 'Underground Camp' was an unusual one, an enlarged fox-earth in a slope of easily dug sandy soil. By a miracle, it never collapsed and buried anyone. The dense tangle of rhododendrons in the highest part of the wood around Six Ways gave us endless amusements in the way of Tarzan-type enactments and games of capture and release* (Alec Scott).

'Haldens Adventure play space, 1967' (*CNT 74/12/1469/29*).

'Fair at Haldens Park, 1973' (*CNT 74/14/KW2832/30*). An early Garden City fair, in 1928, included carousels, slides, swings, 'hitting the bottle', an open-air Punch and Judy show, a Scottish sword dance and a pretty ankle contest.

'Aerial of Area no. 3, showing the Viaduct, 5.9.53' (*CNT B/79/11118/B*). *I can't understand why, during the war, Jerry didn't bomb that viaduct. If he had hit that, he'd have made miles of confusion. There was a loop line, but it was only a single track, and it wouldn't have taken the traffic. That viaduct took millions of tons of traffic. It were never touched* (Walter Broughton). This pre-development picture shows the vast expanse of the north-east area to be built upon. Part of the village of Welwyn is bottom left with Digswell Park Road threading through the viaduct (centre).

'Aerial of Digswell NE area showing Fine Fare and ICI in the foreground 1957' (*CNT C/16.938/B*). The road extending from bottom left of the picture to centre top follows the alignment of old Black Fan Road, its western end becoming The Boulevard, leading into Mundells – before it became the huge one-way roundabout system it is today. The junction with the old sewage road can be seen top left: one resident recalled *they used to have the tomatoes growing there*. Bessemer Road crosses the middle of the picture (left to right), Tewin Road is above it, and the now defunct Hertford branch line mirrors the line of Black Fan Road on the right. *The original Black Fan is not there any more. It was half a dozen cottages and a sewage plant . . . but the cottages are not there and the sewage farm has been amalgamated into what they call 'The Lagoon'. It's got foul water in it. There's still Black Fan Road, but of the original Black Fan, there's nothing* (Walter Broughton). The name reportedly came from 'Black Fanny', a Romany gypsy who was said to have sheltered Dick Turpin from his pursuers.

'Aerial of Panshanger area, 1962' (*CNT M/25019/C*). The three works on the Bessemer/Mundells site includ
Smith Kline & French, with its famous 40-metre tower being constructed. On the bottom right of the picture car
be seen 'northlight' factories, so-called because their north-facing rooflights let in the light but not the heat o
direct sun. Black Fan Road, right, was officially opened in 1965, though it had been used by learner drivers before
then. In 1978 Panshanger residents voted overwhelmingly against a hostel on the corner of Panshanger Drive and
Black Fan Road: it was to be for 27 young men 'homeless because of domestic problems, under the supervision o
a warden', but it went ahead.

'Aerial of Viaduct with nursery in centre, 1962' (*CNT M/25021/A*). Bessemer Road has now extended through the viaduct, Lodgefield has been completed, with works soon to start on Nursery Hill (right of railway line).

'Aerial of Murphy Radio (centre) and ICI (top), 26.6.57' (*CNT C/16.940/B*). Alec Scott worked at the Plastics Division of ICI, *situated alongside the now defunct branch railway line to Hertford, for many years, until my retirement in 1982. From my office window, I could look down on the Social club's bowling green which was, as far as I could estimate, just where I had come across a dead sheep in a field of stubble, about fifty years earlier!* Althea Richardson also worked for ICI: *I thought I'd just work for two or three years as a short-hand typist. There were about 300–400 secretaries working there. Then I discovered that the boss of all that was an old childhood friend. When she retired she said, Would you like to take over my job? So I went from being her secretary to doing her job, and I really enjoyed it. I did it for about eight years, in sole charge of about 100 staff.* Walter Broughton thought highly of the company too: *That was the best job I ever had. I was on the police there, shift work of course. It was well paid and you were well looked after. As long as you did your rounds, kept your eye on everything, nobody bothered you. I was there until I was 65, and I had to retire.* The company closed down most of its complex in 1982.

Frank Murphy had set up his first radio set factory, aided by a staff of seven, in Broadwater Road in 1929. His philosophy – far advanced for its time – focused on his customers' needs and included 'special offers to retailers, fixed retail prices, reasonable but not excessive profits, and the highest standards of service' (Denys Cussins). Workers received two weeks' paid holiday, sick leave, and subsidised hot lunches in the works canteen. All this was considered by some to be 'Murphy madness'.

By 1932 there were more than 1,000 Murphy dealers and 430 in the workforce at WGC, and the company moved to new premises. In 1938 Frank Murphy resigned to form a new furniture company based on 'The New Conception of Business' which, he argued, should 'enable us to express our individuality in the service of others'. The Managing Director of Murphy Radio until 1962 was Edward J. Power, formerly the Chief Engineer. In 1962 the company was taken over by Rank Radio International, until it closed the facility in 1981.

The new Murphy Radio Factory, builder John Laing & Sons, 1955' (CNT A/23105). When Frank Murphy severed his connections with the firm in 1938, then employing 800 people it was because, he told the *Welwyn Times*, 'his personality is no longer willing to be confined within the framework of a limited company.' There were 'limitations' for some of the employees, too: *In Welwyn Garden, I had the opportunity to work for Murphy Radio in its early days. I didn't think so much of it as a firm – I came in as an assembler of radios, but I thought, This isn't my cup of tea. . . . They were just starting their plan of delivering their radios, by road, and they'd got a fleet of vans and I drove them for years. I was a van driver, you see, and I was back on the road again, and I was happy. It was a Union Shop: there were very poor wages in comparison with some of the other firms, so I left. Originally Mr Murphy was a London fellow and he worked for the GPO as a telephone engineer, and he started building sets at home on the kitchen table. WGC was just opening out in those days, and he took this*

*factory ready made. Mr Power – he were Managing Director, he were no good. He expected too much for too little – that's putting it bluntly* (Charlie Green).

Walter Broughton also disliked working for the company: *When I was 13 I went to a polytechnic in London to do precision engineering – for three years. I was awarded a first class certificate in 1931. I had to get a job wherever I could. I got in at Murphy Radio. They were the world's worst employer. They were slave drivers. When it got near the Radio Exhibition every year, in November, they used to build up a stock of sets, and they used to have us working from 8 o'clock in the morning till 12 o'clock at night, all day Saturday, all day Sunday, only flat pay, no time-and-a-half – you just got flat pay. They wouldn't dare do it now. My mother complained at me coming in at 12 at night. I'd say, Well, I can't help it, I shall get the sack if I don't. She said, Well get the sack, I'm fed-up with this! So the following day, I said to the foreman, Can I go at 8 'clock tonight? He said, No you'll stop till we've finished. I said, I'm going home at teatime. He said, You do! At teatime, I got on me bike and went home. Next morning I got an hour's notice – an hour's money – ninepence. I got me dole stopped for six weeks.*

*When Murphy's started up they imported out-of-work Welsh miners to the factory. 10 pence an hour they paid them. Come Christmas time, all these Welsh miners got the sack, just like that. No warning, no nothing. They just pushed them out. And if they'd got any work, they'd come back again in May or June, some of them did. . . .*

*Mr Murphy was quite a nice chap, a pleasant fellow, but he was superseded by E.J. Power – he was a right one he was, hated by everybody. He wouldn't unbend for anything. I was on inspection, I'd always been an inspector, and one day there was one faulty switch. I put it in my overall pocket, so it didn't get mixed up . Somebody went and told Power I'd stolen the switch. He came down and tore me off a strip. I said, Am I going to steal a sixpenny switch? I put it there so it didn't get mixed up. Anyway, he went on and on and on. In the end he went away. That was one thing I remember most. . . .*

'Industry at Welwyn, 1938, Welwyn Foundry' (*CNT 76/17*). This was WGC's heaviest industry, opening in 1927 and lasting into the early 1970s. It was sited on Bessemer Road when it was *a fairly short cul-de-sac leading off Bridge Road East with just a few industrial occupiers: Dawnays, structural steel contractors; Beiersdorf, makers of Nivea Cream; and Welwyn Foundry, producing iron castings* (Alec Scott).

'Aerial of the industrial area showing Norton Abrasives in foreground, 26.6.57' (*CNT C/16.944/B*). The Hertford branch line crosses diagonally top left; Bridge Road East extends from bottom right to above centre where it meets Heronswood (right) and Knella Road. To its left are Norton Abrasives (bottom), Barcley Corsets (centre) and the Royal Exchange building on the corner with Woodfield Road.

'Norton Grinding Wheel, 1952' (*CNT B/PF/7916*). When it opened in 1931 Sir Theodore Chambers, Chairman of the WGCC Board, claimed its arrival came about because of 'the wonderful housing available, and the good social conditions, making for happy healthy workers'. Bill James worked in the packing and shipping department. *He used to come home with his trouser turnups full of sawdust'* (Doris James). John Richardson recalled: *A lot of children were evacuated to the United States in 1940, arranged by the Managing Director of Norton Grinding Wheel. They were taken to Worcester, Massachusetts* (where the company was based). Although the company expanded in the mid-1950s, by 1982 it had to cut back with the loss of 100 jobs.

'Barcley Corsets, 1952' (*CNT B/PF/7916*). *When I was 14 I started my first job at Barcley's. I was employed as a machinist on corsetry using an electric machine. My working hours were from 8 till 5 with one week's holiday a year. The war started and I was called up to do war work in Norton Grinding Wheels, using an electric handsaw . . . my hours were shifts of 6–2 one week, 2–10 the next* (WI member).

'Royal Exchange Offices, Bridge Road, July 1956' (CNT C/7250). *When I was 16 I worked at the Royal Exchange in Bridge Road. It's gone now. I just did office work – to do with insurances. I was a punch-card operator – they're obsolete now. I didn't mind the work [but] the bosses were very bossy. We weren't allowed to move, we had to sit and work, not allowed to speak, not allowed to have private phonecalls. There weren't many men there, mostly women. Our boss was a man – he was a person to be afraid of. A couple of girls upped and left. He would stand at the door and watch you sign in and if anybody was late he used to put a little star against their name. It was horrible. A big fat man he was, used to smoke a cigar* (Joan Lammiman, née Beck).

Joan Beck (centre) aged 16, with her friends outside the Royal Exchange offices, 1957. *We started at 9 and finished at 5. We had a 20 minute break in the morning, same in the afternoon, an hour for lunch. Actually, it wasn't a bad firm to work for: the money was reasonable. At the interview, I was frightened out of my life. I know he looked at my report; he didn't say a lot. I didn't even have to sit a test or anything. He just said, 'Right you can start on such and such.' That was it. On my first day, I had to sit at this machine. Nowadays you get work experience, but then, it was nothing. It was straight into the deep. It was hard at first – I couldn't get anything right. The punchcards were all coded. I thought, what am I doing here?* (ibid)

'Industrial landscaping at Smith & Nephew, Bessemer Road, 1963' (*CNT M/522/20*). *Smith and Nephew were a good firm. I worked there until I retired. I was supervisor there. I worked in the packing depot. . . . Mr Cooper was the boss. It was a big company when I started working for it. You clocked in. I started part-time there, then did more and more hours. When we first went there, they were a rather poor paying company, but suddenly – whether there was some rule come in, I don't know – the wages jumped terrifically. I think that was the time when there were more jobs than people to do them* (Anne Hazelwood). The firm left the factory in 1982.

'Industrial landscaping off Tewin Road near Carnegie Chemical Factory, 1963' (*CNT M/523/25*). The road was developed in the late 1930s when ICI moved in. Off-target bombing hit a factory there in October 1940.

'Sectional Factories, Brownfields, 1962' (*CNT K/L258/4A*). Many small businesses had been encouraged to come to the Garden City, though some exposed employees to hazards. In 1941 a 16-year-old boy was employed by a nearby firm to stamp attaché case locks on a 'Besco' press: 'He was told how to work the machine and to be careful. He put the piece of metal to be stamped in the machine with his left hand, operated the press with his foot on the pedal and removed the metal with his right hand. While he was removing a piece of metal after it had been stamped, his foot came off the pedal, the die came down and crushed his right hand' (*WT*). The firm was fined £25 with *2s 6d* costs.

'Attimore Hall Farm House and Buildings, 1965' (*CNT 74/14/1*). The broken windows and damaged roof tiles belie both the farm's past and its future: now it is in the centre of an industrial area; but when it was farmed by Mr Masson, *most days after school we would walk through the bluebell wood from Hatfield Hyde village to Attimore Hall Farm to fetch milk for mother* ('RT').

# CHAPTER THREE

# SHERRARDS WOOD
# & THE NORTH-WEST

'Children's play space, Templewood, 1966' (*CNT P/1365/22*). During the Development Corporation's first few years its expressed main function was 'to provide homes for Londoners who have found work in any of the town's numerous industries . . . also for essential people like doctors, midwives, transport workers, teachers' (WGCDC handbook, 1963). Other Garden City residents had to wait for their own house, which sometimes forced families to live apart, unless they could find some other way of getting a roof over their heads: *Then we saw this advert in the Welwyn Times looking after an elderly gentleman, and went for an interview. The man took pity on us because we were separated. (So) we lived on Woodland Rise (near Templewood). It was a three-bedroomed bungalow, and we had a large living room and two bedrooms. All I had to do was look after him. He used to get his breakfast, I got lunch and would keep the house clean. He was 80 and very sprightly. My youngest boy was 2 and he used to follow him round the garden – it was a big garden. He thought the world of him. We were there four years* (Dorothy Greener).

Sherrards Wood has reportedly acquired its name from one of two contrasting origins, from *seregg*, meaning bright ridge (where the chalk shows through), or from *sliregg*, meaning watery and deep. Its past has been similarly chequered: the area had osier beds, a hopfield, a vineyard and fields ploughed by teams of eight oxen which created near self-sufficiency in the Middle Ages; yet the Black Death of 1348 brought ruin. Railway engines clattered and puffed through the woods to Luton and Dunstable for over 100 years, their sparks a continual peril along the southern boundary of the wood; yet the line was closed in 1965, all tranquillity once more. In 1927 it was cited by the WGCC as one of the exceptional 'natural amenities of the town. . . . It is in the heart of beautiful countryside . . . delightful woodlands (where) primroses, bluebells and violets cover much of the open spaces in the spring and the nightingales sing'; yet in 1962 an exasperated Development Corporation spokesman told a local reporter that one particular area – 'The Dell' – was 'ravaged by children who ride bicycles over the flowerbeds, slide down the slopes on pieces of corrugated iron, and have even used wire cutters to get in, even though the gate is always open. A considerable sum was spent in 1959 on making this a desirable amenity, and I'm fed-up with turfing kids out of it.'

Children, however, have loved the woodlands as their adventure space for as long as the Garden City has been in existence: *Sherrards Wood was a paradise – during the summer holidays we spent hours upon hours there climbing the trees looking across to Shredded Wheat in WGC. It was marvellous (Joe Weston). We liked to give names to various parts of the woods. 'The Heather Hills' were a more open area where heather grew – long gone now. 'Dead Man's Acre' was a group of dead trees standing among bracken. 'The Spy Tree' was a very tall pine which could be climbed to a height only limited by your nerve. It commanded a view over the whole town and we called it the tallest tree in the whole woodland. Two steep hills on one of the trails we named 'Crocodile Hill' and 'Alligator Hill'* (Alec Scott).

'Youth foray into Sherrardswood' (*WGC handbook, 1946, courtesy Joan Lammiman*).

'The Dell: a natural open-air theatre in Sherrardspark Wood (*sic*)' (*WGC handbook, 1930, courtesy Ann Adams*). This famous picture shows *the perfect setting for an open-air theatre, especially Shakespeare's* As You Like It *and A Midsummer Night's Dream. It was often used by the town's amateur dramatic groups. Its only drawback was the occasional noise of a train rattling by on the branch line. . . . The photograph was taken round about 1929. At the foot of the sloping rows of seating is a group of three small boys – Jack Goody, Rick Goody and me (Alec Scott). In the woods there was another dell . . . an overflow of the reservoir came down to it. In wet weather, there was always water in it, and of course it was glorious for young boys. We used to get old oildrums, big ones, and make rafts and sail on this. One time, I must have been about 12, I was on this raft and went over into the water. We lived at the time in Russellcroft Road. I rushed home, over the railway crossing, and mother took one look at me, and put me in the bath. I said, Gosh, my knee hurts, and mother could see that it did. What had happened was that when I'd fallen off this raft, I'd jabbed the knee with an old rusty nail. She immediately called an old friend who was a doctor, Doctor Miall-Smith who lived nearby, and she gave me an anti-tetanus jab. This dell . . . was called 'Ledge Camp'; the boys used to call it that because above was a ledge dug into the ground. You could sit on it and smoke cigarettes. We didn't but some people did* (David Goode).

At the birth of the Garden City the wildlife in Sherrardswood Park was said to include fallow deer, foxes, polecats, badgers, weasels, stoats and a dark shrew mouse with a white saddle; more usual now are rabbits, shrews, mice, voles, moles, grey squirrels and hedgehogs. The birds included jays, nuthatches, tree creepers, tawny owls, little owls, green and spotted woodpeckers; in summer there were willow warblers, chiff chaffs, blackcaps, garden warblers, cuckoos, whitethroats, turtledoves, tree pipits, and fly-catchers; other visitors included nightingales, nightjars and wood wrens as well as the currently numerous blackbirds, thrushes, robins, wrens, dunnocks, tits and finches. All this was such great temptation to little boys in the 1920s and '30s: *I regret to say we indulged in bird-nesting [though] we took great care never to damage a nest and always left two eggs uncollected* (Alec Scott).

'Brockswood Lane, commencing no. 10, 1927' (*CNT A/MT/1483*). The road, once a 'mere cart track', wound steeply through open cornfields – *what we called the 'ups-and-downs'. My mum used to keep chicks in the front room in cardboard boxes to keep them warm. We got them from a place called 'Day-old Chicks' in Brockswood Lane* (Ted Hazelwood). Other locally known residents included Dr Miall-Smith whose *first surgery was in her living room. She was our family doctor. You had to wait in her dining room* (Althea Richardson); and Patrick Heron, 'one of the (most) important British painters of the 20th century' (*The Guardian*): *as wartime conscientious objectors 60 years ago, he and I, along with other awkward customers, were put to digging bog-oaks out of the Cambridgeshire fens* (Alec Scott).

'Bridge Road, Old Cottage' (*CNT B/13B/16*). This famous old house, no. 39, is the Garden City's oldest, built in 1604. The Halsey family lived there at the turn of the century from around the 1820s: 'Both inside and out alike exhibit that harmony which is the secret to all beauty . . . vistas and views ravish the eye from various points in each room and the whole house is a veritable sermon in wood and stone on the text: "In this house I will give thee peace, saith the Lord".' ('PPP', *WGC Pilot*, 1924). The road used to be known as Hunters Lane, a cart track, with Sherrards Wood coming right down to its edge. Two ponds either side often merged to make it impassable.

'Bridge Road 4.4.67' (*CNT P/1466/77*). In one of the 18th-century Handside estate cottages lived Cyril Starr. His *family predated the Garden City and were of old Hertfordshire working class stock, and so we lumped in Cyril Starr with the 'Peartree Kids', the enemies from 'the other side'* (Alec Scott). Joe Weston arrived in WGC at the age of 5 from a *little village in Cambridge where I was fostered out as a boy. I went to my mother's in 54 Bridge Road. Miss Coe* (the much-feared Handside School headmistress) *lived across the road from us. There were six of us in our family. If Miss Coe was in her garden on a Sunday afternoon, we would tiptoe past. She'd say, Hello children! and we'd say, Yes Miss. She was good. She loved children.* Bridge Road had the town's first pumping station and fire station. It was the second road to be constructed by the Company, and had the town's only paved path. In 1934 6 Bridge Road burnt down: this wooden hut 100 ft by 15 ft had been built in 1921 alongside the temporary Estate Office where the police station was later built; it housed the first parish meeting, the early services for pioneers held by Hatfield Hyde's Rev. Jasper B. Hunt, and the baptism of the Garden City's first baby, Evelyn Setters. Tenants included the Workers' Educational Association, *Welwyn News* – and Mr Hyatt's furniture shop, destroyed in the blaze.

Sherrardswood School, 1931 (*courtesy David Goode*). The school opened in 1928 with three pupils in a private house in Elmswood. As it grew bigger it transferred to a new building just north of the Campus. *It used to be known as High School; it was just over the White Bridge. My parents sent me there and it was a happy free atmosphere, run by two ladies, Miss Wragg, the headmistress, and Miss Grimshaw* (David Goode). The picture shows the schoolmaster, Mr Pitt (left) and Miss Grimshaw (right). Other teachers remembered at the school included *Miss Coventry – 'Covvie' – was quite a character: she used to ride a bicycle, very nice lady, but a 'Miss'; Mr Carlson – he was a great chap, he had a motor bike; and the next headmaster was a man called Annand and his wife* (ibid). David Goode is in the middle of the front row. Along with children from families of the pioneer creators of the Garden City – Louis de Soissons, Richard Reiss and Frederic Osborn – other pupils at the school included the sisters of the playwright Joe Orton, the grand-daughter of H.G. Wells, and Dinah Sheridan, the filmstar daughter of the Royal Family's photographer, Lisa Sheridan: *Of course all the boys thought she was marvellous, and absolutely fell for her* (ibid).

During the Second World War there was a voluntary evacuation of two-thirds of the pupils to Worcester, Massachusetts. The first group of 39 children and 4 mothers left in August 1940. By 1946 the school's advertisements for 'a modern school for boys and girls from 5 to 18' augured a bright post-war future; so it was front-page shock news when, in 1954, Sherrardswood School was reported to be closing. It had severe financial problems, with the school losing £4,000 a year. 'We . . . have shown that boys and girls who fail the 11 plus can nevertheless be brought up to university standard,' argued Tom Heron, Chairman of Governors, in a plea for support. Eventually its future was secured when Digswell House was used as a boarding school, £13,000 in donations was promised, £18,000 was given (by donors like Norton's) – and staff offered to accept cuts in their salaries.

Later, the school severed its physical links with the Garden City when it moved to Lockleys, reportedly because a sports ground with a house was needed for its development.

'No. 4 Densley Close' (*CNT B/6/5*), *c.* 1950. This interior, photographed as a 'pre-war building' by WGCDC, was in a home off Sherrardspark Road near Roundwood Drive.

'Roundwood Drive, owner-occupied housing in the early development, 1970' (*CNT S/2137/9*). Near here was a brickworks where there was a *pit about 30 ft deep; the clay was hauled out by a cable up a steep light railway track. There were several brick kilns, each about the size of a small cottage, and a tall square chimney. And there were wide settling beds where the washed clay was kept to mature. . . . It was in one of these that I came to grief one autumn day. I stood on the edge; the clay was concealed under a carpet of dead leaves. . . . I took it for firm ground and stepped on it and was instantly immersed up to my armpits in clay the consistency of custard. I forget what my mother said when I got home, and it's just as well* (Alec Scott).

Walden Place, 1930 (*courtesy Ann Adams*). The WGC handbook caption for this picture reads: 'an instance of simple architectural design round open front garden'.

'Walden Place – pre-war building' (*CNT B/B5/4*). This picture was probably taken in about 1950, the pathway having been widened to accommodate cars.

'Aerial of the Digswell area, 2.6.55' (*CNT A/13974/B*). The main railway runs along the right side of the picture with part of the village of Welwyn above centre right. The development around Great Dell (centre left), Knightsfield and The Vineyard (centre right) and northern Digswell Road is just beginning. Coneydale stretches across the bottom third of the picture to meet Digswell Rise (right).

The gap in the Coneydale houses through which Digswell Road is now advancing was made *courtesy of the Luftwaffe* (Alec Scott). Two houses were completely destroyed in 1940, with nearby Mandeville Rise also affected. Althea Richardson remembers: *I went to school the next day, and I was going to have tea that day with my new little friend, and she didn't come to school. I said, Why hasn't she come to school? Eventually somebody told me, her parents were killed last night. . . . The little girl and the evacuees were thrown out and only had broken ankles . . . a baby was put under the stairs in the next house – everyone was told that was the safest place – and they put him there and he was killed.* The local newspaper report was circumspect, for security reasons: 'Thursday 3rd October 1940: A town in South East England. . . . Three adults and a 7-month old baby were killed, one by debris piercing the roof . . . [There was] magnificent ARP work. One resident, Mrs Lowe, was awakened by the noise of a plane, got the children downstairs and was then thrown on her knees by the force of the explosion. Her house was badly damaged. . . . The ARP arrived within minutes and they worked like trojans.'

Across the top left corner of the picture is the line of the Great North Road whose stories are the stuff of legend: nearly 300 years ago, while Robinson Crusoe's author, Daniel Defoe, denounced it as impassable, the highwayman Dick Turpin used it as a stalking ground; a little later, while stage-coaches still laboured along it, it featured in the novels of Dickens and Austen; later still, early Garden City adventurers ensured its romance persisted: *Digswell Hill on the old Great North Road (now the roaring A1(M) motorway) was where we would collect glow-worms from the roadside and place them on our school caps [for] cycling home in the dark from The Clock swimming pool in Welwyn* (Alec Scott).

'Coneydale, photographed after landscaping had matured, *c. 1950*' (*CNT B/B13F/p19*). ICI *had no. 1 Coneydale where I started work in 1948 – we had this lovely big house, and it had its own tennis courts, three floors and a lovely medlar tree in the garden. . . . Digswell Rise was where the Directors had their place* (Handside Neighbours Club member). *Behind Coneydale, there was a large gravel pit, driven into the hillside and served by a short branch of the light railway. Round the top of this pit was a field of scrub where many bushes of wild briar rose grew. We cut the long strong stems, valuing them more highly than any other wood for the making of bows. Hazel rods were used for arrows, and we called the field 'The Happy Hunting Ground'* (Alec Scott).

'Digswell Road, spring 1959' (*CNT G/JC/74*). This view was taken just before the bend at the modern Pentley Park junction, south of Coneydale.

'Digswell Road 1961' (*CNT K/JC/DC/134*). Every year Corporation photographers (this one was John Chear) would take a shot of this view of the Digswell Road from the junction with Coneydale – the pedestrian subway is halfway up the hill – presumably for comparison. These are two in the sequence.

'Digswell Road, May 1964' (*CNT N/788/30*). Now, in 1999, the view can no longer be seen – the trees completely mask the houses.

'Aerial of the UDC Scheme 17 roads and sewers, Digswell, 26.6.57' (*CNT C/16.929/B*). Looking south, the photograph shows the main railway crossing the left corner with the Shredded Wheat factory amidst the industrial area top centre. The Digswell Road has been advanced to join Bessemer Road, bottom left; the developments of Harwood Hill, Byfield, Haymeads and Burycroft (left) are nearing completion. To the right of Digswell Road can be seen the start of developments for Kirklands, Shoplands (with its pedestrian subway) and Knightsfield. The latter does not yet cross the railway, but the existing pedestrian bridge to Lyles Lane can just be seen above centre. The development started here is The Vineyard: *[in] The Vineyard area, there was a little farm [with] a cart-track. They used to have a bull tethered just this side of the hump-backed bridge* (Avis Westlake).

'Digswell Farm buildings, April 1958 prior to redevelopment as a community centre – Vineyard Barn' (*CNT G/JC/DC/44*). *We used to go for walks on Sundays to the Digswell Farm* (Handside Neighbours Club member). A more vigorous leisure activity was pursued by young boys: the *'best, fastest and longest'* illicit ride on the light railway rolling stock started from near here, according to Alec Scott. Half a mile long, the track ran down to the gravel pits on the Hertford Road at Digswell. *Many a spectacular collision or derailment was contrived, and I do not understand how no-one ever got injured or even killed. Or, for that matter, how we failed to end up in court.*

'Mr C. Gordon Maynard (Chairman of WGCDC) helps Mrs Jean Reed to open the door of the Digswell Lodge Farm Social Centre, 23.5.59' (*CNT 75/24/p14*). The old barn was converted into the main hall, and the cowman's cottage was changed to committee rooms and a kitchen.

'Underpass, Digswell Road, 1961' (*CNT L/JC/DC/113*). Haymeads is in the background. The subway is seen looking east from the direction of Shoplands.

'Aerial of the extreme North West, Digswell under construction, 1959' (*CNT L/21112/A*). The viaduct (top right) shows Bessemer Road emerging underneath, meeting the top of Digswell Road. Digswell House is left, above the newly scoured beginnings of the Oakdale development, bordered by Monks Walk, centre left. New roads for Pentley Park and Templewood are bottom right.

'Shoplands, 1962' (*CNT K/13541*). The shopping centre opened in 1960. *The world and the bus route ended at Shoplands*, recalls Tony Rook. There were no street lights and no surface on the road when Knightsfield residents tried to negotiate their way back *in utter darkness. You could get to Welwyn and the nearest cinema via what the OS map called 'The Avenue', WGC called 'Crossway', and everyone else called 'The Row o' Trees'. Merle (Rook) cycled home along it one night and straight into a deep trench kindly provided by the contractors* (ibid).

Shoplands, 1999 (*author*).

'Official opening of Vineyard Barn Association Social building at Shoplands by R.H. McNab 28.10.67. Committee Room, left to right: Dixie Lee, Bill Jarman, Sally Rogers, Eric Taylor, Paula Jenkins, David Hanchett, Kay Mowbray' (*CNT 74/12/2193/16/VB1-9*).

'The Viaduct Health Centre, November 1966 (*CNT P/1364/18*)'. In 1927 the town had three dentists and four doctors – one of them Dr Miall-Smith. *She had a tremendous influence on the town – she opened the town's first Family Planning Clinic which always amused her because it was in a hall which belonged to the Roman Catholic Church – she would have to cover up the altar and put all the what-have-you on top* (Althea Richardson).

'Digswell Park Conference House and 14th-century Church of St John the Evangelist with Welwyn Viaduct in the background, 1930' (*courtesy Ann Adams*). The 1805 Digswell House was a soldiers' hospital (1914), a Conference Centre (1928), an ICI Directors' Guest House (1939), part of Sherrardswood School (1954), an Arts Trust (1959), and private housing (1987). *A small but troublesome negotiation (in 1919) was with the occupant of Digswell House and Park, Colonel A.D. Acland, who . . . bitterly resented the sale of the land by auction as he would have bought the park himself if informed in time. . . . He could not reconcile himself to 'a horde of yahoos from London' and before long . . . he departed to some less infested place* (F. Osborn).

'Aerial of New Town Area no. 3, 3.9.1953' (*CNT A/11120/B*). *I got into trouble with Digswell House – that was rented out to Colonel and Lady Acland. Every time she came to the village all the boys were supposed to bow to her and the girls were supposed to curtsey. Well, some of us thought we'd rather didn't do it and we got into trouble for it. Some of them did because their fathers worked for the estate – they had to do it. But me and two others [would] go and hide. My father was a signalman, [another's] was a carter on the railway and the third one was a harness maker. We were always getting into trouble for not bowing, although the schoolmistress was more on our side than she was on theirs* (Walter Broughton).

'St John's, Digswell, 1957 – the oldest part is 12th century' (*CNT G/JC/DC3*). Freda Schaschke, newly married to Frank in 1930, wrote in her citizens' handbook by a picture of St John's: 'This is the church we often go to'. Although Yorkshire-born, the Schaschkes made their home in the Garden City for a year or two around 1930. Mrs Schaschke looked after the children of Major Povak who lived at 10 Digswell Road where 'all the newest houses' were. She later resided in Ravenstone, near Milton Keynes in Buckinghamshire, where her daughter, Ann Adams, found the book after her death in 1996.

Walter Broughton giving a talk to pupils of his old school, St John's School, in 1990. *I was there until I was 12 (1926). There were three teachers in the school- one for the babies, two for the others. The infants were in one room, the rest of us were all in one room, divided across by a curtain. Standards 1, 2 and 3 were presided over by Miss Parram, commonly known as Granny Parram – she looked it too! . . . Granny [had] a long skirt down to her ankles, hair done up in a bun, cardigan pulled up tight, belt with keys on it. She could teach though, she wasn't a bad teacher. You didn't have chairs then. You sat on forms in rows. If Granny thought someone wasn't paying attention, she'd throw the chalk at them, and she seldom missed* (Walter Broughton).

'Monks Walk, 1957' (*CNT G/JC/DC27*). *There was a small empty and derelict reservoir which could be seen near the top of Monk's Walk – perhaps part of the water supply for Digswell House* (Alec Scott). *A chap called Cookson who ran the Riding Stables [from what is now] the Backhouse Rooms, part of the old Handside Farm, had some land near Monks Walk. (During the war) I was told I had to plough it. . . . Now Cookson never stood any nonsense – as Major Cookson in the First World War, he used to send people over the top. I started ploughing, and this very irate man came across the field, waving a stick at me, red in the face, big bushy moustache he had. He got up to me and I stopped the tractor, and he started banging the mudguard very hard with his stick, saying, Get off my bloody land! I said, Well I've been told I've got to plough this. He said, If you carry on, I'll go back and get my gun! So I telephoned Headquarters and they said, Well you've got to plough it. . . . I said, But he'll get his 12-bore out. He didn't mess about, old Cookson. In the end, one of the managers came out and thought we'd compromise in some way and said we'd leave a bit of land at that side* (Ralph Parkes-Pfeil).

'Conference House from Knightsfield, 1964' (*CNT O/JC/DC/163*). *Two rows of houses faced one another across what became, eventually, a grass plot, which ended at the fence of the Conference House grounds. We were part of a social experiment; at either end of each row, the Corporation housed 'professional' people and in between, 'working class'. . . . The experiment didn't last long* (Tony Rook). *I've been chased, clipped across the ears. . . . Mr Throssell's farm where Knightsfield is now – we were chased by him for climbing up the hayrick* (Joe Weston).

'Road heating, Knightsfield, 1961' (*CNT K/K81/25*). *On the north-facing hillside where an ice house was situated, there are many depressions, about 15 ft in diameter and 6 ft deep – presumably old chalk pits. If you should drive along Knightsfield and wonder why the road suddenly swoops steeply down and up again in the place they call 'The Big Dipper' the answer is that the town planners in their wisdom drove the road straight over a chalk precipice! Presumably, the planner in his office drew a nice bold sweep for the road with the aid of a map that gave no clue to the obstacle. Heating elements had to be installed under the road surface so that traffic could climb the slopes in frosty weather!* (Alec Scott).

'Knightsfield heated road in snow, 2.1.62' (*CNT K/K26 p14*). *In the woods, on the steep chalk slope looking towards Digswell House, was the derelict ice-house which had once belonged to the big house. It consisted of a short brick-built tunnel running a short distance into the hillside and leading to a dome-shaped structure where ice collected in the winter was stored for later use in the kitchen – a sort of primitive refrigerator. We called it 'The Haunted Cave'. Dotted about that part of the woods were quite a few shallow wells with brick surrounds, one of them roofed with a wooden structure* (Alec Scott).

'Uplands, November 1963, with an unmade road. First on right: flat nos 123–29; first bungalow on left, no. 118' (*CNT O/KW705/14*). Nearby, Nick Faldo (as a carpet fitter) lived in Redwoods, later in Ayot St Lawrence in a house once owned by Gerry Anderson of 'Thunderbirds' fame. In 1978 at the age of 20, Faldo won his first major golfing victory, the Colgate PGA at Royal Birkdale.

The same view, 1999 (*author*).

'Monkswood at play, 1969: a natural play area' (CNT R/1964/18). *In the springtime the meadow to the north of Templewood was a great sheet of cowslips. Some of the grass remains between the woodland and the Knightsfield housing . . . in the middle of that meadow there was a large chalk pit with a shed and some mature trees. The eastern edge of the pit was a sheer 20 ft face of chalk [now the 'Big Dipper'] where we sometimes used to look for a jackdaw's nest (Alec Scott).*

'Aerial of Templewood, 1960' (CNT L/21940/A). Knightsfield is top left, running into Great Dell; the beginnings of Pitsfield (left centre), Pentley Close (below) and Nut Grove (bottom left) issue from the curve of Pentley Park with Templewood itself extending down the right side of the picture.

# CHAPTER FOUR

# HANDSIDE & THE SOUTH-WEST

Lawrence Hall, Applecroft Road, Handside, c. 1930 *(courtesy David Goode). This is quite a famous photograph: it is the clinic where the young mothers used to bring babies to be inspected. Health in those days was very communal – my mother worked there weighing babies. That was a Friday afternoon they had this clinic (David Goode). You went to Lawrence Hall in the 1930s to see the dentist – you had a blue card for a boy and pink for a girl and you stood there with a towel over your arms, waiting for something to happen. There was a washbasin at the side for you to spit in. They did nits at the same time – Nitty Nora, the nit lady used to come round (Rosemary Mitchell).* Funded by Letchworth's wealthy Miss Lawrence, the Hall had a number of functions. Initially it housed many film shows, the first of which took place in October 1922: 'A splendid programme has been arranged. . . . It is hoped that this innovation will be given the support it deserves as the new venture cannot succeed without the hearty intervention of the public. It will be several months before there is a Hall set apart for Pictures and this is a praiseworthy attempt to fill the gap. Mr J. Herbert Williams Mus. Bac., FRCO, LRAM, will preside at the piano and the music, though easily appreciated by the man in the street, will never be blatant or trivial.' *(WT, 1922). Later it was a little school and in the evening it was a place of entertainment – a social on one Saturday night, a whist drive and a dance on another (Doris James).*

The original village of Handside – previously known as Haneshyde (1400) and Hauntside (1838) – lay around the junction of Handside Lane with Bridge Road. It was just a collection of cottages, inhabited by agricultural workers, centred around a water pump from an old well – the town's only public supply of water until 1923. There were no shops, church or public house – unlike Hatfield Hyde in the south-east, the Garden City's only other indigenous community. 'Handside was the last place God created and never quite finished!' said W.J. Horn (of the local farming family).

With the onset of the Garden City, however, the area around Handside Lane and Applecroft Road became over the years a cultural and social honeypot for all age-groups: for example, a Library and Reading Room was an early creation at Upper Handside Farm; Miss Marjorie Bailey, *tall, willowy and incredibly refined*, ran her School of Dancing from Applecroft Road; the Lawrence Hall counted among its many users the St Francis Church Boys' Club, run by Mr Mackness (known as 'Mackie'); and even cowsheds were converted to become the Backhouse Rooms in 1923, named after Edward Backhouse who was killed in a climbing accident in the Alps in 1922. Rosemary Mitchell's father used to help teach gym to 'Mackie's boys' in this same hall; it now houses the Handside Neighbours Club (run by Rosemary and her husband Brian Mitchell), which was started by Police Sergeant Cyril Hughes 'for the benefit of all the adult inhabitants of the south-west corner' in February 1958. It now has a membership of nearly 50 members, many of them over 80 years of age, who enjoy speakers on topics from fantasy eggs to bee-keeping.

'PT display by St Francis Boys' club, 1951' (*CNT 73/18/12*). Alec Scott recalls: *The St Francis' Church Boys' Club met weekly in the Lawrence Hall. . . . I belonged to it for several years, but the club's activities were somewhat limited, consisting entirely of physical exercises and boxing. Clad in white singlet and shorts, we were drilled and marched about, and performed a kind of rhythmic dancing to piano music . . . . Mackie organised an annual seaside camp for the club, but I never went, preferring the Scouts' summer camp, which offered more varied pursuits.*

'Applecroft Road, 1962' (*CNT K/13607*). This road has a number of 'firsts' to its name: in 1921 it had the first de Soissons-designed houses to be built in the town; no. 2 was the residence of the Garden City's first police constable, PC Lee; and in 1923 the town's first elementary school was built here too, known originally as Handside Primary School, Applecroft Road.

Alec Scott has much to remember about the Head of the Junior School there: *the infamous Miss A.M. Coe, and I don't use the term 'infamous' lightly. Seldom can there have been a person less suited to be a teacher. She was a short, stocky woman with iron-grey hair and a slight Scots accent. Built like a pillar-box, with a mouth to suit, straight across with no discernible lips. She had a profound hatred of children, especially boys. Her permanent mood seemed to be one of sullen, simmering fury, occasionally breaking out into terrifying rage.*

*There were two boys who lived just across the road from the school, and their names were Nelson and Napoleon Potter.* (see p. 26) *Their mother was a gaunt and formidable woman, about 6 ft tall. Nel and Poly Potter were not the best behaved of pupils, and consequently, they became acquainted quite frequently with Miss Coe's cane. When this happened, Mrs Potter would swoop into the school like a Harpy and seek out Miss Coe, wherever she might be. There ensued a shouting and screaming match, widely audible. Often they would carry out their discussion in the corridor running alongside the classrooms. In this case, the lessons in the nearest room had to come to a halt, while the teacher and pupils sat in nervous silence. One of the combatants was tall and bony, the other short and squat, but there was little to choose between them in respect of venom and malice. I have a suspicion that each relished the encounter a little. Eventually the tumult and the shouting died down, and class work could resume, uncommonly subdued. . . .*

*When I tried for a Scholarship to Alleyne's Grammar School in Stevenage . . . Miss Coe did her level best to destroy my self-confidence. I can still hear her hissing in my ear in her Scots accent, 'Ye haven't the ghoost of a chance!'*

'Aerial of Handside Playing Fields and Tennis Club courts, 1962' (*CNT M/25029/A*). The curve of Applecroft Road is top right with Handside School top centre right. Handside Lane crosses the top third of the picture above the playing fields, left, and Barleycroft Road, right.

In 1930 the doomed R101 airship passed over the town. Alec Scott was among the schoolchildren of Handside School who were trooped out to see it just days before it crashed in flames near Beauvais in northern France. *It looked like a huge silver cigar, apparently moving quite slowly, and the sound of its engines was very distinctive – a deep throbbing rumble.* Another recalled: *I was born in 1926. In 1930, when the airship came over, I remember I was upstairs in bed and the doctor had come to see my mum about something and all of a sudden he come running up the stairs and said, She must see it! It'll be a sight she'll never forget. I remember him bringing me down and showing me* (Handside Neighbours Club member).

Ralph Parkes-Pfeil comments: *Handside was a tough school in those days, before the war. I failed my '11 plus' at Parkway so I went to Handside. Jimmy Nichol, the headmaster, was a friend of the family. When our parents went on holiday to France, I went to stay with them. When I got back to school, we were gardening one day and I stuck a fork in someone's leg, whether accidentally or on purpose, I don't know. I had to stand outside the Headmaster's door – it was a serious thing. I thought, that's all right, I won't be caned because I'm a friend of the family. But I was caned; it didn't make the slightest bit of difference: there was no favouritism.*

'Elm Gardens and mature trees, 1964' (*CNT O/JC/DC 172*). There are many reminiscences about this road and for Elmwood, opposite Elm Gardens:

*The Cottage Hospital was originally in Elm Gardens (1923–40) before it was transferred to Church Road* (Rosemary Mitchell).

*Between the west side of Elm Gardens and the houses of The Links, there used to be a quite high cliff of gravel, accessible before housing was built. I plainly remember trying to dig a cave in the gravel face – a foolish trick which luckily did not end with my entombment* (Alec Scott).

*When I first started school, we went to a little school at the end of Elmwood run by a Mrs Haggis. She had two teachers for about 12 of us. I didn't like it* (David Goode).

*I was only about 3½ when I started my music lessons and I had them with Mrs Haggis. . . . She and her husband and daughter were the first people to come to WGC. They arrived in a horse-drawn caravan, the very first residents of the town. Mrs Haggis set up a music school . . . she had her grey hair piled up on top, and wore long dangly earrings. She would rap my fingers if I went wrong – I was 3½! – and by the time I was 4, I had given my first concert, but I did it all wrong* (Althea Richardson).

*I came to WGC in 1938 when I was 13 as a refugee from Vienna in Austria and I've lived here ever since. I lived in Elmwood with Mr and Mrs Hughes. It was four days before Christmas when we arrived in the Garden City. We had snow then. I came from Dover Camp and they asked people all over the country if they would take people in for the duration. Gradually the children were dispersed here, there and everywhere, and this particular day Mr Hughes and about half a dozen others came to a London station – I forget which – and we all stood there. There were loads more children and gradually they all went, with Gerda and I standing there and he kept looking around – he could speak very good German, and Gerda could understand a bit of English. He said, I don't know what we are going to do. Apparently the lady who was going to have us had changed her mind, so he brought us down here and took us into his house. . . . Mr and Mrs Hughes seemed very old, upper middle class, had a study, a violin. The daughter was nice, about 19. She was training to be a nurse, played the piano. She would say, Do you want the radio on? You can have it on for half an hour – Geraldo, you know – but don't have it on any longer my dear, I can't stand the noise! I felt a bit like a fish out of water. I can't tell you how I came to learn English, but they were so kind* (Sonja Pooley).

'Attimore Road, interesting for its open front gardens, *c. 1929*' (*courtesy Ann Adams*). *The town ended at Attimore Road in the '20s. South of that were open fields except to the east of the lower part of Handside Lane, there was a large poultry farm . . .* (Alec Scott). George Lindgren lived in nearby Attimore Close *and he went swimming every day early in the morning down at Stanborough Pool all through the year* (Marjorie McBride). *Chairman of the Council in 1933–4 [he] became Lord Lindgren, Minister in the Labour Government of 1945. He founded the WGC Swimming Club. As late as the 1960s he could be seen jogging down to the pool in shorts and plimsolls. I often had a cheery Good morning! from him as he jogged by* (Alec Scott).

The same view, 1999 (*author*). Upper Handside Farm used to be known as Bull Attimore Hall and Farm, near Bull Raffing Common, now the site of Attimore Road. In 1925 the first 'all-electric' houses were begun. In 1954 two houses in the road (nos 28 and 30) were struck by lightning which 'looked like a ball of fire . . . bringing down the chimney-stack, cutting the telephone, blowing fuses and showering soot into the rooms'. One Smith family from Elmwood witnessed it, another Smith family in Attimore suffered it (*WT*).

'Attimore Road, photographed after landscaping had matured, *c. 1935*' (*CNTref B/12B/15*). *I lived in Attimore Road. It were a lovely road. It were a beautiful house. It was laughable how it all came about. We lived at Redbourne, so I said to the missus, Come on we'll enrol for the Garden City. After a while I went in to the Housing Office to see about my application. He said, Ooh, that's going back a bit. He got my application down and blew dust off it. He said, I'll get you fixed up. About a month after, he said, I've got you a house. If you don't want it, there's no need to have it. It was in Peartree Lane. There was the school and then these little old concrete houses. I did not like it one little bit! We turned it down . . .* (Charlie Green).

'Attimore Road, 1962' (*CNT M/13570*). *. . . Then after about another month he said, I've got just the ideal house for you in Attimore Road, and do you know, it were beautiful! When you opened the door, it said Welcome! It was a council house, and Attimore Road, of course had more houses for sale. It was no. 30. I was there for 38 years. The reason I had to leave was I've got glaucoma. I'm 93 now. For about 10 years after I retired I was sighted, then gradually . . . I [became] practically blind. They had some stairs [in the Attimore Road house] and I fell down the stairs twice, suffered facial injuries, so the doctor said, They're building some new flats in Peartree Lane. I'm going to get you one of them, and we went there* (ibid).

'Youngs Rise, 1927' (*CNT A/MT/1480*). Workers' houses were built in 1921 in Elm Gardens, Applecroft Road and Youngs Rise 'to try and prevent an east/west divide'. In 1924 an enraged Youngs Rise resident wrote to the *Welwyn Times* about a plague of flies at the dump near Elm Gardens – 'battalions of them within a few hundred yards of three residential roads, a nursing home, a group of Council Cottages and last but not least, an large and increasing school . . . an *up-to-date* city without an incinerator, and *up-to-date* city with a plague-spot in the near vicinity of many houses and a school – is this a legitimate claim?'

'The same view, July 1955' (*CNT A/MT/1471*).

'Valley Road, looking towards the Garden City commencing no. 52, 1927' (*CNT A/MT/1479*). Miss Hawke, a teacher at the Handside Junior School (now Applecroft), was killed in a road accident here in the late 1920s. *'White Lady Pit' was near the foot of the road – a small gravel pit which was named on account of the alleged sighting of a ghost there* (Alex Scott). *Our mother was very dramatic. She woke me up one night, late at night. She said, I want you to see this! and she dragged me down out of the house onto the grass verge of Valley Road (where we lived in 1940) and she said, Look! and the whole sky was red – that was London burning . . .* (Althea Richardson).

'The same view, 1955' (*CNT A/MT/1470*). *One afternoon, after a particularly severe bombing raid on London, I remember seeing a middle-aged [couple] carrying a suitcase trailing down Valley Road looking completely exhausted. I was at our front gate, and they said, 'Is your mother in? . . . Have you got room in your house to give us somewhere to sleep tonight. We've been bombed out. They had been to the Council offices, and they could not find a corner of the Garden City to put anybody. They said, All you can do is knock at people's doors and see if they can take you in. Mr and Mrs Molder . . . had to sleep in a single bed, but they were very, very grateful* (Althea Richardson).

'The Welwyn Garden City Golf Course: 18 holes near Brock's Wood, *c.* 1929' (*courtesy Ann Adams*). The 'Newtown Trust Field' near the Great North Road was reported to 'open for golf in 1922 for 2 guineas subscription . . . for the sort of golf one plays on Christmas Day', according to its captain, Richard Reiss. His house overlooked the green belt where the new golf course was laid out. He was a keen sponsor of all sports, encouraging them actively by donating challenge trophies and arranging loans. *By the golf course there was bracken going down to the railway, and we used to light fires and cook potatoes and onions in the open and sit in camps – you know the sort of things boys do – but today lighting a fire is forbidden* (David Goode).

'WGC Golf Links, 1956' (*CNT JC/DC/4*). An ancient Belgic tribe farmstead site was built on Brickwall Hill, later known as Brickwall Farm, where the golf course is today. *The slopes of the golf course were the accepted location for tobogganing. After the [nearby] brickworks had been closed for several years, a few friends and I made good use of some of the heavy copper strip forming the lightning conductor of the chimney. During a snowy spell we decided to make sledges . . . the one absolute essential for a toboggan is the metal strip. So one moonlight night we set out to the deserted works with ladder, rope and hacksaw, and detached a sufficient length of copper strip from the chimney. Our sledges were a success* (Alec Scott).

'Carnival, 1970 – Digswell Nursery entry for CNT – Linda Douglas, Jennifer Jones, David Coster, Terry Down' (*CNT 74/13/2276/26*). The Digswell Nurseries were started in 1921 to provide trees, shrubs and flowers for the Garden City, a resource imitated by later New Towns. *We moved up to Brickwall Nurseries (Digswell Nursery now) when I was 8. We had a landmine drop behind us. Our cottage was all damaged. There was a great big hole there. The apple trees had all been blown around. . . . We had a big clock up on the wall, and my dad had to stand on the chair to wind it. When we heard the first bomb drop at Brocket, he said some naughty words. The next thing, all our house crumbled in and the blast blew the door in* (Florence Weston).

'Brocket Close, 1927' (*CNT A/MT/1477*). The *Welwyn Times*' report of the same 'bomb from a Nazi raider' on 21 November 1940 relished this 'remarkable escape from injury. Tiles were torn off the roofs, windows smashed and doors blown off by the force of the explosion. Greenhouses and glass frames suffered severe damage. An apple tree in the orchard was uprooted and came to rest on a barn, the roof of which was damaged, some distance away. Mr A.R. Webster, who resides at the cottage, his wife and daughter aged 13 were in a downstairs room preparing for bed when they heard the explosion: "I was winding up the clock when I heard what I thought was heavy AA gunfire. I then heard a crash and the windows caved in and glass flew all over the place."'

'High Grove, 1927' (*CNT MT/1482*). This is one of five closes, among the earliest developments of the Garden City and accessible from the triangle of Brockswood Lane, High Oaks Road and Valley Road; the others are The Valley Green, Brockett Close, Dognell Green and Dellcott Close.

'Dellcott Close, July 1955' (*CNT MT/1564*). Alec Scott lived in the Close in the '20s and '30s. The residents he recalls include *a Dutch businessman, a courtly, gentlemanly type and very good amateur pianist . . . a neighbour's teenaged daughter slipped on a polished floor and broke her leg which had to be amputated — the whole town was shocked. . . . Mr Drover, the Close's official gardener, a lean ruddy-faced smiling man with a shock of frizzy grey hair [who] when issued with a motor mower, approached it circumspectly, as if fearing that it might run away with him – as it did once, ending up in a rose bed. . . . Councillor Wyvil August, a very snappy dresser with blazer, silk choker, immaculate flannels [and] a four-seater open Minerva with a polished aluminium body.*

'Dellcott Close, 1929' (*courtesy Ann Adams*). Another resident, *Mr Limb, [owned] the Bickiepegs factory in Broadwater Road – hard teething rusks for infants, advertised as 'The Food of Royal Babies', [which each] had a ribbon attached as a precaution against it being swallowed. Mr Limb used to ride a primitive forerunner of the moped, a bicycle with a small and unreliable petrol motor attached. To start the machine, it had to be pedalled before the engine fired. Mr Limb pedalled almost as much as he rode. The Bedells family [were] socially very OK indeed – they had two cars and a distinguished visitor, Captain 'Tim' Birkin* [winner of the 1929 Le Mans in a supercharged Bentley], *who would roar down the Close in one of his enormous cars* (ibid).

The same view, 1999 (*author*). *Milk was brought round in a churn on a two-wheeled horse-drawn trap, taken out in a cylindrical pint measure with a hooked handle and ladled into the housewife's jug. A greengrocer from Codicote, Mr Dollimore, came with his horse-drawn cart, a lugubrious looking man with a bowler hat and a big walrus moustache, eloquent in describing the juiciness and flavour of his fruit: Mrs Dishwashins 'ad some o' these and she said they was lovely, he once said, referring to the wife of the chief architect of the town, Louis de Soissons. Sometimes a travelling knife-grinder appeared [with] a strange contraption which could be pedalled like a bicycle then somehow unfolded to become a pedal-driven grindstone* (ibid).

Handside Lane, 1929 (*courtesy Ann Adams*). *Handside Lane was a track. It was a paradise* (Joe Weston). The Handside Farms became a natural cradle for the new Garden City in its infancy. Early 19th-century landowners had imported farmers from Scotland and descendants of these immigrants were still the 1919 tenants of Digswell, Brickwall, Peartree and Handside farms when the Garden City was designated. Most of them objected to being dispossessed by an unscrupulous set of 'city-slickers'. Frederic Osborn recalled: *They need not have worried. Beside them as business bargainers, we were babes in the wood.* They remained *pretty unfriendly* except for the Horn family of Upper and Lower Handside and Brickwall farms, whose land was the first to be taken over for development. An affectionate limerick of the 1920s commemorated them:

> Three generations of Horn
> Handside Lane on fine mornings adorn
> County Alderman (grand-dad)
> Parish Councillor (dad)
> And a young motor bicycle Horn (Osborn P)

In the early years of the Garden City newcomers found a 'New Town Hostel at Lower Handside Farm [which] provides accommodation for men and women engaged in professional or other work' (WGC residents' guide, 1926). Doris Siserman got a job there for 15s a week *with all my food and a very nice room. . . . Many of the people staying there were Quakers and vegetarians who came from Letchworth. . . . There was a big well in front of the hostel and a very big bucket which was filled up with meat, bacon, butter and milk and let down the well to keep the contents nice and cool.* One of the boarders refused to help her lift it because he was vegetarian.

During the war young Jewish refugees were housed in the hostel 'lent by the Reiss family': W.M. Lash, one of those who escaped from Germany wrote: 'What greater merit can be bestowed on a man than to proclaim that . . . R.L. Reiss wrested 20 lives from the hangman [and has] given them back their lives, faith and hope in humanity.' A factory manager of Handside Lane 'could not in clear conscience take part in any combatant military service as it was a direct violation of the Lord's instructions'. His Chairman confirmed he was 'already performing service of national importance since the firm were producing steel doors for air raid shelters, roof trusses for militia hutments and guard rails for municipal trenches'. He was duly registered for non-combatant duties.

'Garden of 131 Handside, c. 1950' (CNT B8/7). *Four sisters lived on the corner of Handside Lane, daughters of a Professor of Philosophy from Glasgow University. The eldest was on the first Brains Trust with Joad and Huxley. The second was Sarah Walker, an artist. The third was a character, the fourth was a librarian and very clever. They were brilliant conversationalists. I learned from them that the art of conversation is to listen* (David Goode). 'What women want', declared an advertisement for Handside in 1926, were 'tiled floors, slow combustion coal grates, a modern boiler, an enclosed dresser with cupboards underneath, glazed tiled hearths, easy-clean taps, smooth-surfaced kitchen doors, a linen cupboard, tiled bathroom, and gas fires in bedrooms.'

'Mr Hussey of the Commission's Forestry Department sorts it out: a Russellcroft Road tree in 1969 and Sir Frederic Osborn' (CNT R/1918/25). In 1924 a Russellcroft Road resident, Lily Collier, made her house a collecting point for the charity 'Relief for Germany' to help children 'in urgent need of feeding, absent from school through lack of clothing and shoes. . . . Surely they are not guilty of anything that brought on all their trouble?' (WT).

'Guessens Road. Guessens, meaning guest-house, is the name of the house in Old Welwyn where the poet Edward Young lived' (*courtesy Ann Adams*). The road had its own celebrities however: Sir Ebenezer Howard lived at no. 5; Sir Frederic Osborn lived at no. 16; and members of the Women's Luncheon Club which met in the Guide Hut from 1934 to 1941 included wives of famous husbands, considerable activists in their own right: Mrs Crowley JP, co-founder of the Hostel; Mrs de Soissons, Home-helps organiser; Mrs Reiss, co-founder of the Cottage Hospital; Mrs Nichol, MP for Bradford North. Their talks included Vera Brittain on 'Women in Transition' and Dr Edith Summerskill on 'Italy under Fascism'.

The same view, 1999 (*author*). In 1937 Miss Jane Savory became supervisor for the Guessens Road Nursery School: 'I have found the Garden City children differing most strikingly from those in London and South Wales on the one hand in their far greater responsiveness to adult suggestion; their complete lack of shyness with adults; their preference for individual play as opposed to playing in groups; and the high degree to which their powers of reasoning are developed. On the other hand, their powers of imagination and sense of independence are relatively undeveloped.'

'Guessens Road: one of the many pleasing groups of houses owned by the Urban District Council, 1929' (*courtesy Ann Adams*). Built for workers in 1924, they were demolished in 1970, having been '*of a noticeably lower standard than most of the housing to the west of the railway. Some had no separate bathroom, just a bath in the kitchen with a wooden lid, [nor any] electricity supply in the upstairs rooms* (Alec Scott). *These were tiny little terrace houses with pretty large back gardens in keeping with Ebenezer Howard's ideals of having green space. One of these little houses, known as 'the 'ouse' by its resident, Mrs Wallhead, the elderly mother of Muriel Nichol MP, was completely demolished by a bomb* (Althea Richardson).

'Guessens Court: an inside glimpse, 1929' (*courtesy Ann Adams*). This was originally a co-operative housing scheme of flats with a common kitchen, dining, reading and recreation rooms, laundry, garden and tennis courts. Rosemary Mitchell remembers *listening for the ring of the dinner bell of Guessens Court Hotel (now residential flats). This was the 7 o'clock signal for me to go indoors for bedtime. I lived in Lanefield Walk and the hotel backed on our garden.* Doris James, Rosemary's mother, spent most of her married life in Lanefield Walk: *It was a working class house all right – no bathroom; the bath was in the scullery opposite the gas stove. The loo was just outside the back door . . . and no electric switch upstairs – you had to come downstairs to switch it off. We had a huge cherry tree. When we first moved in it was about 12 inches high. We had moved it to the top of the garden and it grew to a massive size. We used to have Sunday tea under it in the summer. There were masses of cherries but the birds always ate them first. We retired in 1966 and were informed the same year*

*that all the houses were to be demolished and the tenants to be offered bungalows. There were meetings of protest, but it didn't make any difference. Bill was very disappointed because he was going to do so much in the garden when he retired . . . it was heartbreaking to leave the old house . . . they were there for a couple of years and many were vandalised, but in the end they were demolished.*

'Barleycroft Road, housing built mid-1920s, July 1959' (*CNT G/62*). Jack Major lived with his parents, Billy and Daisy in no. 33. To the boys growing up in the new Garden City, he was *our acknowledged authority on the identification of a bird or nest and also something of a rebel: for some years he added excitement to Guy Fawkes Night with a home-made firework. He mixed potassium chlorate, flowers of sulphur and sugar into a paste with a small banger as a detonator . . . it was heard all over town like a thunderclap. Once it was placed on top of an old oak gatepost which was reduced to splinters, and once he took it to Sherrards Wood where he placed it in a metal litter bin among trees close to Six Ways. After the explosion the litter bin had vanished and the surrounding trees had shreds of steel embedded in their bark. We were just juvenile delinquents who got away with it* (Alec Scott).

'The Old Barn, Handside Lane (the theatre is now part of the original farm), winter 1965' (*CNT O/JC/DC/184*). Dame Flora Robson appeared here as a young amateur actress. C.P. Purdom, father of film star Edmund Purdom, and the Company's Finance Director and MD of the Stores, wrote, produced and acted in plays there. The WGC Film Society moved here in 1952, the same year that the film studios (see p. 50) closed down: *The auditorium was cold and draughty or stiflingly hot. Running film shows with one 16mm projector (was) a tricky and hazardous operation. Disaster did strike . . . but the audience noticed only a sudden removal of the image from the screen, coupled (once) with an audible explosion of profanity from the projection room* (Fred Aicken).

'The Old Drive: formerly the carriageway to Upper Handside Farmhouse, 1929' (*courtesy Ann Adams*). The Garden City's Library was housed there in 1927, but visitors had to endure a dark walk in wellingtons, encountering rats on the way.

'Meadow Green, showing how a setting of fine trees may reconcile diverse styles of architecture, 1929' (*courtesy Ann Adams*). The *Daily Mail*'s 'Ideal Village, a hamlet of new ideas' had 41 houses in 16 designs, 'an irresistible combination of the utilitarian and the eccentric'. Features included the 'Receivador', to take tradesmen's daily deliveries; Crittall metal windows; a 'Wifesjoie' one-ring gas cooker; a Doulton porcelain enamelled cast iron bath; a 'Rock Safetee' gas geyser; and 'Domestikatum' hot water supply apparatus. The infant Alec Scott called to an *old man with snow-white hair and flowing whiskers* who performed the opening ceremony. He was Earl Haig. *I doubt whether anyone with so much slaughter to his account has ever been hailed as Santa Claus.*

'Aerial 1959: swimming pool (centre) with River Lea, Great North Road (right) and Stanborough Lane (top)' (*CNT L/21119/A*). Stanborough School (top left), originally known as the Grammar School, opened in 1939 just as war was declared, with Headmaster James Nichol, *'old Nick, the one with the mortar board and outlandish accent, the most belligerent and hot-headed pacifist!'* Pupils were *often subjected to "gardening" lessons we shifted and levelled tons of a gruesomely yellow mix of sand, gravel, flinty subsoil and builders' refuse [until] we were close to mutiny* (Edgar Rogers). In 1960 Merle Rook, introduced as 'one of those working wives we have heard so much about', felt *totally unprepared for those bleak corridors, serious gowned masters and, paradoxically . . . the air of laissez-faire.*

Stanborough swimming pool, *c.* 1945 (*courtesy Ted Hazelwood*). *In 1935 the town's first properly made swimming pool was opened. It was on the same site as is occupied by today's fine pool but it was a pretty primitive affair. The sides were of wood and the bottom was shingle and the water flowed in directly from the Lea, after passing over a simple bed of gravel which, in theory, removed the larger detritus. The water was always excruciatingly cold and swimming under water with one's eyes open was like being immersed in a thin soup* (Alec Scott). *The changing rooms were all wooden ones, and they had holes in the back where the boys used to peep through* (Anne Hazelwood). *The girls' changing rooms were off the road, and you walked along to get to the entrance and of course as you walked along, you'd look. The river came in one end and went out the other. The pool had railway sleeper-type edging – very slippery* (Ted Hazelwood). *There was a sharp bend in the river Lea [which] created a pool of slow-flowing water, wide and deep enough for swimming. . . . Mr Goody, father of two of my friends, lost his false teeth there in the water and was unable to find them in the mud of the river-bed . . . perhaps they are still there to baffle some archaeologist a thousand years hence!* (Alec Scott).

'Stanborough Lake opening, 19.9.1970' (*CNT S/2305/13*). *During the excavations for the lakes I was walking on one of the spoil heaps and picked up a broken polished flint axe head of Neolithic date. I still have it with the grid reference, 226118, and the date of finding, 25 September 1970. I often wonder about the man who was using it when it broke – the cutting edge was clearly ruined by striking a stone, maybe 4,000 years ago. Was it a major disaster for him and his family, dependent as they were on such tools for clearing trees and cutting firewood? A new polished axe head would take hundreds of man-hours to fashion* (Alec Scott).

'WGC Police Station bar, 1962 (*CNT M/14183*)'. *Down where the police headquarters are there used to be a farm down there* (Handside Neighbours Club member). During the Second World War there also used to be an anti-aircraft battery on the site and below it, at the junction of Stanborough and Lemsford Lanes, a gun emplacement with a multiple Bofors gun and a huge 4.7 inch AA gun manned by *'bored artillery men for whom the exodus of senior girls from school was the highlight of their day. They used any moving object as an aid to gun-aiming practice . . . you never quite got over the shock that you and your bike were being tracked by an enormous piece of artillery'* (Edgar Rogers).

'Aerial of completed houses at Marsden Green, the Football Club ground, part of Handside playing fields (left), and the stadium site in background 26.6.1957' (*CNT C/16.974/B*). The Territorial Army Drill Hall (bottom right) was home to a miniature range used from 1945 by the Home Guard Association whose CO was Lt. Colonel Sir W.H.D. Acland of Digswell House. It also housed WGC citizens 'in appalling conditions' in the early 1950s because of WGCDC's expressed prime purpose to house Londoners first. Lemsford Lane (across the bottom right corner) is remembered *seventy years ago . . . as a narrow country lane bordered by hedges. It was known as 'Tinker's Hill' and the tinker was said to have been John Bunyan who sometimes preached there. Up to about 1932 Tinker's Hill was the boundary of the Company's land and the limit of its jurisdiction over building . . . a motor mechanic named Toplis who had worked for Jenner Parsons set up a service and repair garage in wooden buildings [alongside] where the pathway now leads to Stanborough Park and the swimming pool. He shared the premises with Pickering and Hale — builders and undertakers. Toplis was a first class mechanic and he thrived. . . . Almost opposite the end of Handside Lane close to the present Lakeside School there was a pair of small shops: a small cafe called 'The Corona', and a watchmaker called Forty* (Alec Scott).

'Bulldozer School at Stanborough Gravel Pit, 1945' (*courtesy Joan Lammiman*). *About 1930 [the pit] was used as the location of a film about the war, entitled 'Tell England'. Sitting in school in Applecroft Road, we heard loud explosions of simulated shellfire; our teacher said, I don't know whether they are telling England but they are certainly telling us! We always laughed dutifully at teachers' jokes*. Bill James was driver's mate on a steam wagon for Herts Gravel & Brickworks Ltd there: *they had 1s 6d extra for each load delivered. On a short journey he might do three loads, but a long one, only one. It was a dirty job and he got filthy; he had to bath every day, and our bath was in the scullery opposite the gas stove. But anyway, it was a job* (Doris James).

'Aerial of the Great North Road, Stanborough Road and old Stanborough Lane, 1960' (*CNT L/21923/A*). When a new wooden church was opened by Sir Ebenezer Howard on Stanborough Lane in 1925, it was in 'a narrow country lane separated from . . . the town by cornfields'. In August 1935 'a line of seven defendants stretched across the court at Welwyn sessions', accused of damaging a haystack in the lane by using it as a slide. One, Ivy Branch of Clapton, East London, said they did not go on the stack to damage it but to take "snaps"' (*WT*).

'Aerial of the Stadium area, 1959' (*CNT L/21122/A*). Twentieth Mile Bridge is centre top. In 1920 the dump there was considered a dreadful place, with fires, acrid fumes and swarms of rats and flies. Much of the sand for WGC's construction came from Twentieth Mile Pit, transported by a narrow gauge railway with internal combustion engines. At Chequers (right) Phyllis Parkinson's husband had a coach business: *he built it up himself – Parkinson Coaches – a fleet of four. He used to take the girls from Shredded Wheat to night duty and pick them up in the morning. [My son] built the garage in Burrowfield: we had a heavy steam cleaner there, did our own repairs, it was a beautiful garage. We had our own office, had a lady in the office. . . . It's a junk yard now.*

'Start of the first heat of the 550 yards sprint at the opening of Gosling Stadium, 4 July 1959' (*CNT 73/7/1/12A*). The opening ceremony was performed by the Marquis of Exeter.

'Mrs Beryl Swain, Gosling Stadium, 1961' (*CNT73/8/17/L21830*). The *Welwyn Times* sports reporter described her leading the final, 'her hair streaming behind her helmet,' passing the entire field until her engine stopped from a melted piston. Fred Harris of the Development Corporation is looking on in the background.

'Aerial of Gosling Stadium, 1960. (*CNT L/21925/B*). The stadium was named after the Development Corporation's first chairman, Ray Gosling, who died in 1958. Bricks were made from the gravel taken from the site of Gosling Stadium. *We would have a marvellous time in these bricks, making camps. . . . The engines [from the light railway which transported the bricks] would pull the trucks from the front. They used to have a driver on, but they didn't have a guard, so when they passed any little boys, it was admirable for jumping on. In those days, the whole town was building up – it was so free. Today children don't have this freedom because of the car and control. We grew up in this town very free, and it was happy* (David Goode).

'Stadium Service Station, Stanborough Road, May 1963' (*CNT N/529/29*).

'Des O'Connor in Showbiz v. Team Managers Football match at Gosling Stadium, 10.4.60' (*CNT 73/7/H75/25*).

'Stirling Moss lands at Gosling Stadium, 5.4.61' (*CNT 73/8*). Runner-up in the Formula One Championships 1955–8, Stirling Moss won 16 out of his 66 races between 1951 and 1961.

'Opening of WGC Ski Centre by General Sir Roderick McLeod, 5.10.68 (*CNT 74/13/KW1836/13*).

'Aerial of Stanborough Green and South Parkway contracts, 30.6.52' (*CNT B/7872/B*). Left of the Parkway roundabout (above centre) is Turmore Dale, also known as 'Tommy Dell'. Rosemary Mitchell remembers *collecting mushrooms in the early morning on Stanborough Green and having them for breakfast.* Joe Weston's first impression of Welwyn Garden City was of *all these lovely light railway tracks going all down Parkway.*

'Main entrance to the city, *c.* 1950' (*CNT B4/49*).

The same view, 1999 (*author*). No longer the main entrance, this southern end of Parkway is now a minor exit from the huge roundabout which directs town centre traffic up Osborn Way.

'Parkway School which cost £12,000 gutted by flames', March 1939 (*courtesy Joan Lammiman*). Parkway Schoo was officially opened as WGC's fourth school in November 1934. It was originally to be called Birdcroft School with Miss Alice Coe as Headmistress; she remained until she retired in 1946. Many residents have vivid memorie of her:

*I came to a new school in 1935. I came to Parkway and Miss Coe. I had then a Yorkshire accent which she immediatel said had got to go. I remember her standing me up in the class, and the children laughing at me* (Pat Chambers, né Prior).

*I was sent to the dreaded Miss Coe for a misdemeanour. I believe it was scribbling down the side of an exercise book. was met with the retort, You are nothing but a Hertfordshire Hedgehog! As a 5-year-old I didn't appreciate that one shoul be proud of that fact, not ashamed. I regret to say that I never forgave her and 65 years on I have a corn dolly hedgehog o my mantelpiece as a reminder of that day!* (Rosemary Mitchell, née James).

*I was frightened of Miss Coe. I must have done something good one time, because I remember being sent to her office and I was given a boiled sweet for something* (Dorothea Bagge, née Foggerty).

*When my sister was a pupil under the unspeakable Miss Coe, my mother sent in a quite innocuous note about her schoo work. Miss Coe went into action with her favourite weapons of sarcasm and ridicule. Standing Jean in front of the clas. she made some sneering reference to the note and added, And this child's mother calls herself a teacher! . . . There was or boy, George Barker, who attracted Miss Coe's especial disfavour. Since he was not very bright, she used to make him th butt of her sarcasm. His family was poor, and once he had been unable to attend school for a day or two while his onl shoes were being repaired. On his return, Miss Coe hauled him up in front of the class (I know, I was in that class) an ridiculed him for offering such a 'lame excuse' for his 'truancy'. Some years later, after Miss Coe had taken over the ne Parkway primary school, he burnt it down, was arrested, and did time. He probably thought it was worth it, though* (Ale Scott).

It was more than 10 years before the school could be accommodated under one roof again – classes wei scattered between the Drill Hall, St Francis Hall, The Friends' Meeting House, the Baptist Church, the Free Churc and Lawrence Hall. Some teachers got to their classes by bike! In 1946, it was 'a public elementary school fc children from 5 to 11', and Mr Arthur Worthy became its Headmaster: *What a relief when he took over! He thre open the windows and let the fresh air in. Under him, the school really became a child-centred community where paren and teachers co-operated in their common interest – the welfare of the children* (a parent).

South Parkway, *c.* 1950' (*CNT B/40/106*).

'West side of South Parkway from Honeycroft junction, 1965' (*CNT O/1116/10A*). *The light railway would transport the bricks to all the houses. I played on them. I was in Barleycroft Road which then backed on to all these fields, high with hay, and it was huge fun. You could get into these little wagons and push your sister or whoever down this long thing. I learned to ride a bicycle in the tracks – it was the only place where the grass wasn't too high* . . . (Pat Chambers).

*I remember running to school down the light railway tracks the full length of Parkway; and collecting horse chestnuts outside Parkway School; and taking them home to thread or bake in the oven to make them really hard. . . . Hopefully one would be a winner! On frosty mornings, I remember collecting supple twigs to bend, to shape a frame to collect spiders' webs* . . . (Rosemary Mitchell).

'Interior of 14 Parkway, c. 1935' (CNT B7/6). This house belonged to the Sheridan family, and was where they conducted their photography business, 'Studio Lisa': *A house [14 Parkway] I saw in WGC immediately enchanted me. It was of neo-Georgian design in red brick and had what Dinah called an honest-looking face. The generous portico led into a large hall, the rooms were bright and square, the windows large, and the whole so well thought out that whatever doorway one stood, there was light behind one and before one. There was a feeling of welcome the moment one put one's foot into the house* (Lisa Sheridan). The estate agent refused to let her buy it but then discovered she was a photographer. *He said that the town needed a photographer and that planned towns attempted to attract all the professions that the community might be adequately served. . . . From the commencement of our life in WGC we set ourselves to make records of the town's growth. We have not ceased doing so today [1955]. Town-planners from all over the world come to Hertfordshire to see what has been done, to learn, and to note mistakes which have been made in its early days . . .* (ibid).

Among their many commissions, the Sheridans once used their garden for semi-nude scenes of Adam and Eve: *During the war the house next door was commandeered by the army. We found the entertainment we provided too exhilarating for the soldiers' manners, our work being punctuated by laughter and cat-calls. When we made friends and offered the men certain amenities such as additional baths in our house, and evenings chatting by our fireside, they learnt to respect the way in which others earned their living. Today the house belongs to a dentist whose patients can while away the time watching us. . . . The tradesmen always took an intelligent interest in our work. . . . Our house became an air-raid post during the war, where night and day people reported for duty, and where St John Ambulance men and women rolled their bandages and practised on their pinioned victims every evening!* (ibid).

The family were among the Garden City's first celebrities: *Their daughter was Dinah Sheridan. They had an older daughter called Jill. . . . Lisa was definitely English, though he was not. She was a goer, a great person for getting people to be in the right position. She had all sorts of gimmicks and he was a great photographer* (David Goode).

*They became the regular photographers of the future King George VI. . . . Studio Lisa was granted a Royal Warrant and displayed a Royal coat of arms on the front of their house. From the first they promoted their daughter Dinah as a celebrity. . . . The family were believed to be White Russians . . . this allowed our juvenile imaginations to run riot with fantasies about Bolshevik agents coming to 'get' the Ginsbergs!* (Alec Scott)

'Conservatory, 22 Parkway, c. 1935' (*CNT B9/8*). During the war the WVS's Hon. Sec. Miss M. Pelly at no. 11 administered her 'Civil Defence duties under the Local Authority 1939 /45' which included overseeing a Rest Centre, a Housewives' Service, a Hospital Supply Depot, School Canteens, and the British Restaurant. Another Parkway resident was robbed by his charwoman in 1940 'to buy blankets and food for the baby, and to pay a coal bill and money owed on the baby's cot, and a week's money to the people who were looking after the two children'. The Chairman said: 'You have been a very silly woman . . . you have had a hard time, but you have not tackled the situation as you should have done.' She was bound over for two years. (*WT*)

'Parkway, 1962, where closely mown lawns cost about 1*d* per square yard p.a. and some 30-year-old rose bushes (*sic*) can clearly be seen' (*CNT M/13569*).

'The Roman Catholic Church of St Bonaventure, Parkway, 1929' (*courtesy Ann Adams*). A convent school was run by The Canossian Daughters of Charity from 1922 to 1962 in adjoining buildings: *The nuns wanted my parents to send me here because we were Catholics. I came here from the age of 5 till I was 17. They were very sweet. They taught the whole time to begin with, but then they brought in lay teachers for Maths and English. Although they were Italian ladies, they spoke very good English. It was a fee-paying school: most children who came here were daughters of professional people, so lots of my friends are non-Catholics because they came here. All that remains now is the red-brick house, where the nuns lived* (Dorothea Bagge).

The same view, 1999 (*author*). By 1946 the Convent was taking 'girls from 2 and boys up to 12 years of age'. *Mother Pia, the Headmistress, was very strict: when she walked in the room, there was complete silence. Some 'Nuns of the House' didn't teach at all. They lived there and used to keep chickens and they had a garden which they tilled and they had their own produce. They were a semi-enclosed Order, but not entirely. Certain nuns would go out in pairs to do the shopping. The others all lived in the convent. . . . I have very happy memories of my schooldays. They were very kind, very gentle. You hear some stories of nuns in Ireland who were cruel – we never felt that. They were like angels, gentle, you know, but firm* (ibid).

# CHAPTER FIVE

# THE GARDEN CITY CENTRE

'Welwyn Stores, 1938 (CNT 76/17)'. *I didn't shop in Welwyn Stores – it cost a lot of money. They had a food hall, but it was like the best of food in there. We didn't shop in there. Over the railway line was always called the 'other side'. You'd say, I'm going over the 'other side'. We'd push those big prams, those whopping great prams, for miles over to the town – about an hour, it took. You didn't do it very often. And it was only a journey you undertook in the summer. You'd have another baby on the end of the pram too. You would walk to Peartree, across the field, across the railway bridge – you'd pay a penny and get a platform ticket and walk across the station. You'd go through by Shredded Wheat. I would [usually] shop at Hall Grove. There was a little Fine Fare there. You'd go over the bridge to the 'other side' if you wanted anything different, in the little shops, like there were in those days: there was a nice little knitting shop – the Work Basket, there for years, two lovely old ladies. You could get all your crochet and embroidery. There was a Boots, but mainly it was The Stores, as it was called – you never called it Welwyn Stores* (Anne Hazelwood).

The epicentre of the new Garden City from its earliest days was Welwyn Stores which originally opened on 14 October 1921 on the site of Roseanne House, at first *rather small, only one storey* (Mrs Dalhousie-Young). It eventually included departments for hardware, furnishings, books and boots; and a separate dairy, stationery, bakery, chemist, millinery, creche, hairdresser, subscription library and launderette: *You could get things there that you couldn't get anywhere else. At Christmas the biscuits were wonderful – I've still got the biscuit box! And the fresh fish. . . !* (Handside Neighbours Club member).

The old Stores were demolished in 1939 and replaced by the more substantial buildings opposite the Campus. *I remember when they built the Stores: where it stands now, nothing used to be there. I used to come over occasionally on the push-bike, from Hatfield, and have a look at it. Everybody said it wouldn't stay* (Arthur Clarke). No expense was spared for the new Stores: *There were the most wonderful curtains in the restaurant which were designed by Patrick Heron with Welwyn Garden City motifs – [among them] the storage pillars of Shredded Wheat* (Althea Richardson). Even better facilities were now on offer: *We would go into the Bridge Road entrance of the old Welwyn Stores, roller-skate through the length of the store, bumping down the midway steps as best we could, and go out by the Parkway entrance . . . we would sometimes perform this feat in the summer wearing no shirts, bare to the waist. Oh what desperate thugs we were!* (Alec Scott)

'Aerial of Parkway, 26.6.57' (*CNT C/16.972/B*). Nearly 20 years after its opening the 'new' Stores is still the most commanding landmark of the town centre. Its old site, still empty, is lower centre right, with the Campus complex also yet to be built. In 1984 The Stores were taken over by 'John Lewis, Welwyn' – an unforgivable misnomer for many locals.

'Parkway Cafe, 1938' (CNT 76/17). *You used to go dancing in the Tea Gardens there. On the outside when you turn into Parkway, there was a brown piece with seats there and we used to stand there and watch all the dancing* (Handside Neighbours Club member). *You could sit and have coffee, and you could have a cup of coffee with a choice of either a biscuit or a cigarette – it was 4½d* (Mrs Dalhousie-Young). *I remember going up to the old Welwyn Stores on a Saturday morning, and looking out on the veranda – it was very pleasant. We used to have ice-cream and sit in green wicker chairs. One day, my mother in her folly decided to trust me to [my elder brother's] care. I was about 4. She gave him a shilling for each of us to go and have lunch in the cafe. It was a great event for me: I was going off with my big brother and we were going to have lunch in a cafe! All I remember of the meal is they gave us tinned peas. I think I rather enjoyed them* (Althea Richardson). *The building had a wooden veranda around, and it just made me think of those cowboy towns, you know, where they ride in and harness their horse* (Pat Chambers).

As well as the Cafe, the Stores had an Annexe for films, concerts and meetings (Parkway Hall). George Bernard Shaw gave one of his famed speeches there: 'Parkway Hall was full to the doors. . . . He said, "The sooner they got a theatre for WGC the better. . . . They should do all the acting themselves, and make the dresses themselves and also the scenery. If they found a young lady who thought she could act like Gladys Cooper or a young man who fancied himself an Owen Nares, let them drown the one and shoot the other"' (WT). At a Labour Party meeting in the early 1930s a prospective candidate, 'Mr Brown, a good-looking young man with a nice bass voice', said that the incumbent, Lt Col. Freemantle, had been slavish in his support of the Coalition Government. He was 'an unrepentant supporter of Lloyd-George'. The coalition 'stinks in the nostrils of the electors'. WGC labourers received £2 4s 6d 'for a full week when there were no wet days . . . how would members of the audience like to live on that?' (WT).

George Bernard Shaw himself denounced the 'capitalist monopoly' of the WGCC. However, he had £12,000 invested in it, had his hair and beard cut in its hairdressing department (with awed customers asking Mr Harvey for the trimmings) and was a frequent visitor to The Stores, despite its shortcomings: *When someone went shopping there, they said, Have you got a shopping bag? Everything's on the ground floor (there was only one floor) but make sure you look after the rats!* (Mrs Dalhousie-Young)

'The Cherry Tree Restaurant with its woodland setting, 1929' (*courtesy Ann Adams*). This first Cherry Tree Restaurant opened in 1921 in 4 acres of woodland. Its 'table d'hote' luncheons in 1925 cost 2s 6d. The building was replaced in 1932: 'The last remaining timbers of the old Cherry Tree were removed early last month and on its site now stands the new building almost complete; surely a tribute to the art and skill of the Architect, the Builder, and the British Workman' (*WT*, 1934). You could play bowls (10s 6d p.a.), or at the billiard tables or putting green; or you could go dancing: *Waitrose used to be our dance hall where we all met our husbands. The Cherry Tree used to have nice dances. I remember dancing there every Saturday night* . . . (overheard on bus).

Doris Siserman, 1925 (*courtesy Rosemary Mitchell*). *I met my fate at the Cherry Tree. Being a New Town, all and sundry were arriving, and a number of young men from the Welsh Valleys arrived. I worked at the Cherry Tree for about two years (1926–28) and married one of them. We were together for 60 years* (Doris James, née Siserman). *Phyllis Parkinson also worked there: It was beautiful. I worked on the private side there. Mr and Mrs Gee were the managers. In those days they had a butler, Mr Dibbins – he was always dressed in butler's uniform and had a silver tray. I liked it very much there – it was where I met my husband. He was a chef there, so he courted me for a long time. . . . It would have made a gorgeous hotel – it had marvellous rooms with a bath. The Gees had all the top, and all the staff lived there.*
'Until the late 1950s the pub catered for middle class trade and the restaurant was very popular. As WGC grew, things altered radically and the middle-class custom declined. By the 1970s all of the 20 resident staff had left and the restaurant was closed. Many problems were faced by the pub, including drug trouble and youth rowdyism. The expansion of the New Town sounded the death knell for the Cherry Tree' (Leslie Smith of Whitbreads, 1978).

'The Welwyn Theatre, Parkway, with the first banks and shops in Howardsgate, 1929' (*courtesy Ann Adams*). The theatre, designed by de Soissons, opened in Parkway in 1928 with seating for 1,200. Although its amateur repertoire company soon foundered, it continued primarily as a cinema. One demobbed soldier wrote in 1946 that after being away, he couldn't help noticing that 'we saw better and more up-to-date films in an old Army shack than we ever see here' (*WT*). It housed the annual Drama Festival throughout the '40s and '50s and was regularly used by the film studios for viewing rushes of the day's filming. It became part of Shipman and King's cinema empire, but in November 1962 a serious fire very nearly destroyed it.

'The Welwyn Theatre: modern interior decorations influenced by arrangements for good hearing in the theatre, 1929' (*courtesy Ann Adams*). 'Fire destroyed the stage and . . . much of the interior of Welwyn Theatre in the small hours of Wednesday morning . . . less than two hours after the Welwyn Thalians had rung down the curtain on their first night production of Carousel. The roof blew up; flames shot up to a terrific height and sparks flew everywhere. It was intensely hot: flames came right across the roof.' Firemen from five towns fought to 'stop the flames leap-frogging across onto Cresta's workrooms, the Parkhouse flats and the new telephone exchange' (*WT*). The theatre was later renamed The Embassy, became a bingo hall, closed in 1983, and was demolished a year later.

'Parkway from the White Bridge on Digswell Road, May 1958' (*CNT G/JC/DC/59*). A time capsule was buried under the White Bridge in the late 1920s: *In one of the columns, there's a tin with a newspaper, some money and bits and pieces. I knew the man who did it: it was Fanshaw Watts, Michael Watts' father* (Ralph Parkes-Pfeil). The bridge went over the old Dunstable branch line near which was one of the town's pits for gravel used in its construction.

'CNT landscape returfing in Parkway, 1969' (*CNT R/1632/7A*). *It's changed in the Garden City. People are quite happy to see cars parked on the grass verges – not like thirty years ago* (Ted Hazelwood). *The Garden City has outgrown its town centre . . . parking is a nightmare, and the litter is terrible. We used to have 'Please do not walk on the grass' signs, now they picnic on it* (Ralph Parkes-Pfeil). *They still do these lovely breaks with the trees and shrubs* (Anne Hazelwood).

'Victory Revels: couples waltz on the Campus, 1945' (*courtesy Joan Lammiman*). *About 1920, we used to walk across somewhere where the Campus is now. They dug a big hole in the ground and said, That's where the Welwyn Garden City is going to be started. It was a big hole in the ground and everybody looked down there: a wild rabbit had got in and couldn't get out. We had to leave grass and leaves out for it. It was about 10–15 ft deep* (Walter Broughton).

'Dancing on the Campus, Carnival Week, 1951' (CNT 73/18187). In 1975 the WGC Film Society was invited to move its venue from the neighbouring college to the new Campus West: *Friday nights in the comfortable warmth of Campus West Theatre seemed slightly unreal. At coffee intervals and at the end of each show, we had apparently been visited by aliens – until we realised that the foyer had been invaded by disco dancers. . . . We carefully tip-toed between half-clad Lolitas on the staircase or meandered among copulating couples in the car-park* (Fred Aicken).

'Campus and memorial gardens, *c. 1972*' (*CNT S/2774/9*). An engine shed for the builders' temporary light railway used to stand where Campus West now is. Alec Scott remembers it as a good place for boys to indulge in *illicit and highly dangerous play with whatever rolling stock we could find. We liked a good clear downhill run for riding on the heavy steel trucks. One ride was down through the woodland where de Havilland College now stands. The line ran straight through the car park of The Cherry Tree restaurant and continued along Stonehills and Longcroft Lane. On this run, we had to be careful that the points just before the car park were set to divert the truck into a heap of sand, to avoid wrecking some unfortunate motorist's car.*

'Arrival of HM Queen Elizabeth the Queen Mother to celebrate WGC's Golden Jubilee, 30.5.70. Her Majesty is on the dais' (*CNT 74/9/2193/16*).

'The Campus, autumn 1971. Bronze by Kathleen Scott (Lady Kennett of Dene). In the background, Campus West Amenity Centre under construction for WGC UDC' (*CNT P/FCW/WGCPS*). Colin O'Connor, who worked on the Campus West building site remembers that one of the workers *fell from the top of the building on to sand – and lived!*

Campus West was the site of the first building yard in the Garden City when the WGCC appointed as its contractors for road work and housing Messrs Trollope and Colls Ltd. Early in 1920 they constructed a camp of old army huts for 200 building workers who had to be brought in from outside. Sir Frederic Osborn recalled that 'this had a canteen and a shop . . . in the charge of a lively character called Budge who must have been a capable manager because there were never any serious signs of discontent. He was also the compère and a leading performer in the camp's evening entertainment: he led the crowd in what may rank as WGC's first folk song:

> Trollope and Colls, Collop and Trolls
> They're not related to Sally Joel's
> Never invented sausage rolls
> Or SOS to save our souls
> Trollope and Colls, Collop and Trolls
> When the grave-digger the bell he tolls
> I'll cover their graves with scaffold poles
> If I live to the finish of Trollope and Colls.'

The building achievements of the Garden City's first 10 years – 'figures that talk' according to the WGCC in 1929 – were certainly impressive: the number of houses 'completed and building' had increased, like the population, by 30-fold – 8,700 people now lived in 2,540 dwellings, worked in 45 industries, sent their children to 9 new schools, and went to 7 churches and 11 meeting places on 20 miles of road. All this was not achieved, however, without some discomfort for the men who were engaged in their creation: in 1922 the workmen's camp was denounced for its 'insanitary conditions . . . a workman tells you he has slept nine weeks in sheets which had been used when he took them over' (*WT*). The camp was demolished in 1923.

'The 1951 Summer Carnival' (*CNT 73/18/2*). On opening the Carnival, George Lindgren MP acknowledged the 'old WGC people – the enthusiasts and the propagandists – who were prepared to put their ideals into practice and who had many problems and difficulties to face'. At this point, 'the uniformed youth organisations sounded their bugles and hoisted the Union Jack' (*WT*). Events included a horticultural show, a male voice choir concert, the ICI Plastic sports, and a motorcycle and car gymkhana. 'In the background, the sight of a busy refreshment van and – yes, it must be admitted – some litter on the green, was oddly attractive. For of course, everyone knew that the face of the Garden City would be just as circumspect when all the jollities were over!' (*ibid*).

'The 1951 Summer Carnival' (*CNT 73/18/19*). 'It was crazy . . . two wild savages (Graham Lindgren and Gordon Smale) practically naked except for their colourful warpaint searching for a sacrifice to the beauty of the Festival Queen. They found it in Harry Wilson who had thoughtlessly come dressed as an explorer' (*WT*).

'Carnival procession of Festival Week, 1951' (*CNT 73/18*). The original caption for this picture includes an interesting example of how meanings change: 'Spirit of Carnival sends town gay'.

'Tidying up the Campus, 1945' (*courtesy Joan Lammiman*).

'Fretherne Road and Stonehills, 1965' (*CNT O/1171/26A*). *There used to be the police station in Stonehills and Parsons and the garage. . . . The Co-op was on one side, Boots on the other . . . Dickinson's and Adams was on the corner opposite The Cherry Tree; and Munts, the cycle and toy shop, was right along there . . . [their] bikes had a little saddle across the cross bar where you carried the kids* (Handside Neighbours Club members). *I worked at Munts. It was a nice shop. I enjoyed working there [but] I decided I wasn't making any friends – there was a cycle repair bit at the back and they were men obviously in there* (Anne Hazelwood).

'Shopkeepers' footpath displays, July 1973' (*CNT 75/15/KW2855/8A*).

'Shops, offices and car park, Church Road, 1962' (*CNT K/13526*). The Cottage Hospital moved from Elm Gardens to Church Road in 1941. It was next to the Free Church and was originally Fretherne House School, a private school for boys run by the Rev. Mr Whalley. *My dad was a gym instructor at that school* (Rosemary Mitchell). It may have been 'the local maternity hospital' where a matron enthusiastically partnered Studio Lisa in a commission from a Viennese psychologist to photograph 50 baby faces at the closest possible moment to birth — to prove theories of how a child 'showed his true inherited temperament and that his reactions to birth varied in accordance with his innate character, registering clearly on the face of the new-born child'.

'Millionth visitor to Church Road Car Park, 9.3.71: Mrs Molly Tucker of 40 Attimore Road is receiving a bouquet from Miss Sheila Taylor, typist of the Engineer's department' (*CNT 74/13/2363/28*).

'Coronation Fountain, February 1963' (*CNT M/437/36*). The 1953 coronation was celebrated in wind and rain by street parties and a 25-mile cycle race. *When the jets were turned on, the water rose in magnificent symmetry* (Kirk Robertson). *It was the first 'opening' of a public fountain I've been at where the jets were not set awry and did not spurt the spectators with cold water* (Arthur Cornner, WGCDC's senior engineer). *The winter after our daughter was born was the very cold one, when the fountain in Parkway froze. Fuel was a problem. . . . I would go out in the snow with a saw in a sack and meet others similarly equipped. As well as judicious pruning, we took away a great deal from some derelict stables which were due to go anyway* (Tony Rook).

'Advertising kiosk, Howardsgate, with Wigmores North in the background, 1961' (*CNT K/JC/DC/133*)'. In 1929 the *Welwyn Times* praised the new convenience of tarred roads and paved footpaths in Howardsgate, and the new buildings of the Midland Bank and Barclays. *When the film studios made 'Brighton Rock' I was standing outside the bank where I worked and Richard Attenborough ran up one side of Howardsgate and back down the other, and that was supposed to be Brighton . . . they just pieced it all together so you don't know* (Les Westlake).

'Howardsgate, showing pre-war buildings, *c.* 1950' (*CNT B/WG002/B3*). *Russell Jones was in Howardsgate. He was my husband's solicitor. Next door was a baby linen shop. They had lovely baby clothes in there – a big doll all dressed up. Jack Edwards was next to my sister's shop in Howardsgate. During the war she was manageress at W.E. Turner, next to Lloyds Bank. She used to go and relieve all the managers who went on holiday. Her name was Miss Constable. There used to be a little old lady in the Work Basket . . .* (Phyllis Parkinson).

'Mrs E.M. Berry, (right, with white handbag), daughter of Sir Ebenezer Howard at the unveiling of his Memorial in Howardsgate, 16.7.64' (*CNT 74/6/874/20*). The Garden City's main shopping street was named after Sir Ebenezer Howard – 'a City clerk turned Parliamentary shorthand writer with a passionate interest in social reform and the quest for a "true ideal for living"' (*You magazine*, March 1994). The original memorial – a plain brick wall which caused much controversy – was unveiled in 1930, but was damaged by vandals in 1949 and replaced by this memorial stone in 1964.

'Betsy for teas and home-made cakes', c. 1946' (courtesy Phyllis Parkinson). This picture of Betsy is exactly how it was when I went to work there – only part-time while the children were at school – [from] 10 till 2. I was a waitress in there. It was a lovely tea-shop. You had little coffee-coloured aprons. Mrs Dalgleish (who ran it) was a lovely Scotch lady. Before, it had been a bakery; they used to make their own bread in their ovens at the back. We had one or two film stars in Betsy's, from the film studios. Flora Robson used to come and have coffee and cream cakes. She was very nice. You could tell people of culture (Phyllis Parkinson).

The same shop, 1999 (author). Mrs Dalgleish had it really beautiful there. She lived on the top. Her husband was a doctor in Parkway. She was in the WVS. 'Betsy' was next to the gas office and Pritchards, the sweet shop (Phyllis Parkinson). Betsy's Ltd had started in 1946 and changed ownership from Mrs D.E. Dalgliesh to Reg Simmons in 1954, under whose name a café still trades.

'Stonehills, the new Pedestrian Way, 1959' (*CNT G/KW/G59*). *We used to roller-skate past the shops, and go where Lloyds Bank is, turn left. It was always great fun to 'Keep Out Of The Way Of Sergeant Parker!' He was a big man with a black moustache and he was a great character in the police. If ever Sergeant Parker caught you, you'd get a real telling-off, and he would make us take our roller-skates off* (David Goode).

'Stonehills car park, 1956' (*CNT C/JC/DC/1*)'. Before the stores and the car parks were built, Stonehills was the site of the first WGC cricket pitch, a regular feature of which was a match with Hatfield Hyde Cricket Club. It was also the site of the town's first police station, opened in 1934. The famous Sergeant Parker was its first resident sergeant (until 1938); he had five constables. The building was demolished in 1963 after the new station had opened on the Campus. Stonehills was also the site of a huge bonfire lit on VE day in 1945.

'Aerial of Welwyn Garden City Centre, showing railway and The Cherry Tree Restaurant (right), June 1962' (*CNT M/25026/A*). Pre-dating the Beeching cuts on the railway, this picture shows the still-extant rail of the Dunstable branch line, curving at the top, parallel with Bridge Road. Ted Hazelwood worked as a fireman on the railways from 1946 to 1957: *Going out of WGC there's quite a steep bank. Steam trains had a tendency to slip. If you didn't do it in all one go, you had to halve the train, take half there, come back and get the second half – which means that somebody's got to walk backwards behind the train to put detonators on the line to stop anybody catching you up. If you can't do anything else, you've got to walk to the next station and take the token with you to get assistance to come back and drag you up. So the ideal thing for the fireman to do, because you had sand boxes in front of you, was to put sand on the rail. You'd hang off the side of the train and go along bashing this sand box. But you were happy to do things like that.*

The old railway station can also still be seen, bottom left. *I was very annoyed when they knocked the station building down. I thought it could have been incorporated quite well with the nice columns that it had. You find them all round the garden city, like the Stores, on the 'other side'. I thought it was dreadful. I thought it could be kept* (Anne Hazelwood).

You lovely station of a lovely town,
  Your breadth and cleanliness combine to make
  A beauty that can cause the heart to ache
Sweetly, before the eye can travel down

The glorious gate of Howard, with its crown
  Of green, for very pleasant is the brake
  That closes it, and forces it to take,
For right reward, the symbol of renown.

From a poem by Terence Greenidge, *For the twenty-first birthday of Welwyn Garden City station, 1946* (courtesy of his daughter, Althea Richardson).

'Town Centre, 1956' (*CNT B/22JC/DC/2*).

'Opening of multi-storey car-park, 3.12.73' (*CNT 75/15/KW2925/11A*). 'Station Master Joe Bayliss said goodbye to his station house and garden and made way for progress – demolition of his home for a giant multi-storey car park in its place: "I feel very bitter about having to move, but it's no use fighting it."' (*WT*, 17 May 1963). It wasn't until seven years later that the scheme was finally approved, costing 25% more than original estimates, at £400,000. It opened in December 1973, with 470 spaces on 5 floors.

'Aerial of Welwyn Garden City station, 1959' (*CNT L/21116/A*). The Great Northern Railway London–Peterborough arrived in 1848 along with Welwyn's famous viaduct, 1,560 ft long with 40 arches at 100 ft above valley floor, costing *c.* £75,000 – a mammoth feat paralleled by one of the workmen, Tom Sayers, who was the undefeated English champion of bare-fisted boxing.

The first Garden City settlers were served *by a rudimentary railway station . . . really only a platform and a hut, just north of Hunters Bridge. Commuters, like my father who travelled to work in London, had to change trains at Hatfield for the main line to King's Cross* (Alec Scott). The platform had been built for German prisoners who had been felling timber in Sherrards Wood for a government department *and they were still at it when we arrived. We had to pay a lot of money to save the remaining trees. The railway company did agree, after hesitation, to provide a temporary 'halt' for passengers, but it was another six years before they built the permanent station* (Sir Frederic Osborn). In 1926 the town finally got its own main line station, opened on 5 October by Neville Chamberlain, Minister of Health – but only after the railway companies were convinced it would be profitable. The wide strip of land they owned made all the bridges very expensive – the footbridge opened only in 1936. The problem, according to Osborn, was the provision of a railway station and buildings *on which we had prolonged argumentation with the unadventurous management of the Great Northern Railway who drove a hard bargain with us; we had to sell them strips of land on both sides of the main line at a ridiculously low price. This increased the already wide gap between the west and east parts of the estate, and the length of future bridges, tunnels for pipes, lines, and wires.*

The railway was a dangerous place: in 1934 an 18-year-old porter, employed for only two weeks, was killed at the station while pushing a barrow across the Luton line; a year later the Garden City experienced its worst railcrash, still vividly remembered nearly 65 years on; and in July 1962 one old steam train travelling at speed through WGC left a trail of fires behind it at Twentieth Mile Bridge, Blakemore Road and Knightsfield Bridge, causing a cornfield fire that took an hour to bring under control. Notwithstanding, *it was fantastic to drive a steam train!* (Ted Hazelwood)

Interior of WGC train, 1930 (*Bodley Head*). This picture, part of a children's book created by Studio Lisa, features Jill Sheridan (left) and a carriage interior as might have been experienced by those travelling on the Newcastle express on the night of Saturday 15 June 1935 when a local parcels train struck it: 'Darkness and horror: . . . sudden and horrible death to 14 travellers and serious injuries to nearly 30 more. . . . From the grime and horror of last Saturday night which will be in the memory of those who were there until the end of their lives, the one solace can be taken that the people of Welwyn GC rose superbly to the task before them. . . . Splintered woodwork and twisted steelwork were being manhandled    by firemen and other workers, stripped to the waist with the light of a few feeble oil lamps and torches. . . . Screams and groans from the injured were mingled with the hiss of escaping steam form the two engines. . . . [Witnesses] heard train whistles and brakes screeching and then the noise of the impact. . . . Saturday night was a night of unknown heroes: gifts of fruit, eggs, tea and clothing

were left at the WGC Cottage Hospital by unknown donors.' *My mother heard the crash at about 11 o'clock at night. The first doctor on the scene was Dr Miall-Smith, the sole doctor for some time. She died a few years ago aged about 103. She was a remarkable woman* (Althea Richardson).

'The Flying Scotsman on the last run through WGC, 12.5.68' (*CNT 74/12/1730/3*). *My father used to take me to Hunters Bridge which had a narrow little road with a footpath either side [and] great metal girders on the outside. We would stand there and watch the Flying Scotsman. We were right on top of the steam and the noise* (Althea Richardson). On 4 July 1999 'the world's most famous steam locomotive' ran again through WGC from Kings Cross to York 'after a £1 million, three-year restoration. The 76-year old ex-LNER engine no. 4472 . . . built in 1923 in Doncaster, weighs almost 160 tons and ran about 2 million miles with LNER and BR. [It] recorded the first 100 mph between Leeds and London in 1934' (The *Guardian*, 15 April 1999).

'Bus stop at The Cherry Tree, 1945' (*courtesy Joan Lammiman*). Mr W.H. Washington, first manager of Barclays Bank, remembered the Garden City building going on at such speed that residents coming home in the darkness frequently fell into ditches that had been dug during their absence in town. His first bank building was on the site of the bus shelter opposite The Cherry Tree – affectionately known as the Dog Kennel – and he had to wade to work in riding boots and leggings (*WT*, 1946).

'Part of dual carriageway, Hunters Bridge, 1961' (*CNT K/JC/148*). This link between Handside and Hatfield Hyde used to be just wide enough for two pony traps to pass each other. *Every time we saw the School Truant Officer's car – an old bull-nosed Morris – come over the top of the bridge, we'd dive over the bank, roll down the back and hide in the ditches till he'd gone. He never caught us!* (Stan Scales). *In 1918 Ebenezer Howard took Purdom and me for a day's walk from Hatfield, through Peartree Farm to Hunter's Bridge . . . from which we could see a wide stretch of level farmland without any sight of a building, across Brocks Wood to the Red Lion, and back to Hatfield by the Great North Road. We agreed it was a possible site . . .* (Sir Frederic Osborn).

# EPILOGUE

A key resource for this book has been the words of the people who shared their memories of Welwyn Garden City. It seems fitting to give them the last word. The pages that follow feature just a few of them, who represent the rich variety of its community.

At first, *Welwyn Garden City was the sort of place that if I ran out of eggs, there were about five houses I could go to. I still do!* (Mrs Dalhousie-Young) *And it was safe to play outside – there were no cars coming up and down* (Anne Hazelwood). *Our children used to go out on their bikes for the whole day, take sandwiches – there was no fear. . . . A letter was delivered to me with just my name on it: the place was small then. . . . There was nothing on the 'other side' when we first came – it was fields* (Handside Neighbours Club members). *Everybody was pioneering in spirit and shared the ideas they had – it was very outgoing, I don't know about friendly, but obviously one with a common purpose. The feeling was for the town, and the community spirit was vast. Everyone was interested in other people: there were a lot of altruistic, idealistic people* (Pat Chambers).

*Later, it tended to be that the white collar workers were on one side (west of the railway) and the blue collar workers were on the other. That was a distinct disadvantage of WGC* (David Goode). *The railway line goes down the middle. [On the west side] was where people lived – considered to be the posh part of town. Everything else on the 'other side' was factories* (Mrs Dalhousie-Young). *The awful division of the town, one side of the railway and the 'other' – the industrial side. It sounds awfully snobby from today's point of view, but you didn't cross the railway line unless you had to. It was the blind spot if you like of Ebenezer Howard* (Althea Richardson). *When WGC was designated a new town, that was the start of the change* (John Richardson). *It was terribly snobby in a way – it wasn't meant to be. It grew up and that's why one had a [thing] about people who came later: 'It's our town' – you know how small towns are* (Pat Chambers).

*However, when I was a student, I took on jobs at the Post Office, and I often used to have a delivery round on the east side of the town, and I got to know it – which I didn't really before* (David Goode) *The PO helped us by giving a grant towards removal expenses. We were very happy that we were offered WGC as we had relatives living over the 'other side' – not that this had meant anything to the PO* (Mr and Mrs W.H. Abbott). *I originated from Yorkshire, Barnsley, and I were a bus-driver all me life up there for about 14 years. Barnsley was a colliery area, and I thought to meself – I had two children, a boy and a girl – as I was driving my bus up and down, I couldn't see very much future for my children there. I didn't want them to go down the coal mines or work in a shirt factory or anything like that. I took a long term view of it – I thought when this show's over [the war], there'll be an upset. So I had the opportunity to come down to Letchworth – the first Garden City. I worked there for about 12 months, didn't like it – didn't like the accommodation which they offered. [Then] I came to the Garden City in 1945, just after the war. . . . I've had a beautiful life, I don't regret one minute of it. I was married in 1932, during the recession. England were in the doldrums. We were married 53 years. They say marriage is out of date, but it wasn't for us* (Charlie Green).

*Now, the Garden City is not what it was . . . but it's still good, still a good place to live* (Walter Broughton). *A lot of the older parts, the middle parts, have still got a bit of space round them. I think it's a nice place to live* (Anne Hazelwood). *The Garden City has changed a lot over the years, and I am so happy we moved here all those years ago, a joy to see all the trees and grass everywhere* (Mrs H.D. Gann).

Ted Hazelwood, aged 21, on his 350cc twin Triumph motorbike in 1951. Born in London in 1930, Ted moved to WGC in 1939 and has lived in the south-east area of the Garden City ever since. He has worked on Mosquito aircraft for de Havillands, on steam trains as a fireman for BR, and on the first hydraulic loading shovels for Weatherill Hydraulics. He was Works Superintendent for Hawker Siddeley in Hatfield, Manager for British Shipbuilders at St Albans, and Works Manager for the British Maritime Technology Institute at Teddington, Feltham (where Barnes Wallis used to test his bouncing bombs): he was involved in tests for the *Free Enterprise* disaster, Hong Kong harbour, and a murder enquiry in the London Docks. Married to Anne, he has two sons and four grandchildren.

Another representative of the many contributors to this book is David Goode, aged 24, here commissioned as a Lieutenant in 1947 when he was stationed in Suez. Born in Woodford in 1923, David moved to WGC when he was 3 and lived in the south-west area for 27 years until he married and moved to London in 1953. Conscripted as one of the 'Bevin boys', David worked in the South Wales mines from 1944 to 1946. Graduating from Glasgow University with a degree in Mechanical Engineering, he became a Research Engineer, with one of his projects being the Royal Festival Hall in London. He subsequently joined the oil industry and now lives with his wife in Tring. He has a son and two daughters, and five grandchildren.

'Sir Frederick Osborn on his 90th birthday, August 1975' (*CNT 75/15/KW3152/13*). Born in Brixton in 1885, Frederic Osborn left school at 15 to be a clerk in the City of London. He became a member of the Fabian Society and the Independent Labour Party, and, as a rent collector, experienced first-hand the overcrowded living conditions of tenement dwellers. In 1912 he joined Ebenezer Howard at Letchworth as Secretary and Manager of the Howard Cottage Society. A writer and administrator, he served as Secretary and Estates Manager for the WGCC from its inception to 1936, and as Clerk both to WGC Parish Council and to WGC UDC. A WGC resident for 57 years, he was knighted in 1956 and died in 1978.

Doris James on her 90th birthday, 1997: she was a resident of both east and west sides of the Garden City. Born Doris Siserman in Sandpit Cottages, Hatfield Hyde (south-east), in 1907, Doris lived in Codicote until she moved to WGC in 1923 to work at the New Town Hostel in Handside, and then as a waitress at The Cherry Tree Restaurant. There she met her Welsh husband Bill, and on her 24th birthday they moved into 13 Lanefield Walk, in the south-west area (now demolished) where they lived for 38 years. She bore a daughter, Rosemary, and subsequently worked for Welwyn Stores during the war years. Later she lived for 30 years in Heather Road and after the death of her husband, embarked on an autobiography to tell her daughter 'how it really was'. In 1996 she moved to Hyde Valley House Residential Home, very close to her birthplace, and died there in May 1999, survived by her daughter, two grand-daughters and four great-grandchildren.

# ACKNOWLEDGEMENTS & BIBLIOGRAPHY

The author interviewed and transcribed reminiscences from Dorothea Bagge, Walter Broughton, Doris Bullen, Pat Chambers, Arthur Clarke, David Goode, Charlie Green, Derek and Dorothy Greener, John Hart, Anne and Ted Hazelwood, Peggy Jeeves, Dorothy Johnson, Joan Lammiman, Helga Lomas, Marjery McBride, Rosemary Mitchell, Colin O'Connor, Ralph Parkes-Pfeil, Phyllis Parkinson, Sonja Pooley, Althea and John Richardson, Rene Rowlandson, Betty and Stan Scales, Kate Tibbert, Jean Weir, Avis and Les Westlake, Joe and Florence Weston, Dal Young, members of the Handside Neighbours Club, the University of the Third Age, and residents of Elizabeth House. A huge debt of gratitude is owed to all these kind and welcoming people for their wonderful impromptu stories. The author is also immensely grateful for the eloquent and poignant written memoirs received from: Mr and Mrs Abbott, Fred Aicken, Mrs H.D. Gann, Doris James, Helga Lomas, Rosemary Mitchell, Merle and Tony Rook, but most especially from Alec Scott whose unique style of story-telling deserves publishing in its own right. The verbatim words, written or spoken by all these contributors, are shown throughout in italics.

Special thanks, both for giving the author access to their resources and for loaning them, to Ann Adams, Fred Aicken, Walter Broughton, David Goode, Anne and Ted Hazelwood, Joan and Tony Lammiman, Rosemary Mitchell, Phyllis Parkinson, Althea Richardson, Merle Rook; and particularly to Susan Flood and staff of Hertfordshire Local Studies with their patient and welcoming support; and David Biggs of CNT, now integrated with English Partnerships, whose support in ensuring a continuing appreciation of the New Town phenomenon made this book possible.

Thanks also for their help in smoothing the way to the author's contacts, to Marge Archer of Elizabeth House, Carole Brown of Age Concern, staff at the Homestead Hotel, Ann Jansz, Suzanne Mackay, Brian and Rosemary Mitchell of the Handside Neighbours Club, Michael Pit-Keathley of the University of the Third Age, the Ludwick Wives Club, Merle and Tony Rook, WGC Library staff and the WI in WGC.

Finally, thanks for their help in checking, proof-reading, advising or solving problems to Marge Archer, Walter Broughton, Rebecca Bull, David Goode, Anne and Ted Hazelwood, Bob Hill, Tom Hill, Penny Hutchinson, Doris Martin, Rosemary Mitchell, Althea Richardson, Alec Scott; and for their computer wizardry and calm to David Evans, Sam Hill, Jason Matthews, Michael Rowlinson.

*Alphabetical Guide to WGC 1927*, WGC Bookshop; Brian J Bailey: *Portrait of Hertfordshire*, Robert Hale, 1978; Edmond Barraclough: *Woodhall Lane United Reformed Church WGC 1923–1973: a brief history*; Robert Beevers: *The Garden City Utopia, a critical biography of Ebenezer Howard*, Macmillan, 1988; *Citizens' Handbook*, 1946; Eve Davis: *Within Living Memory*, Countryside Books, 1992; Roger Filler: *A History of Welwyn Garden City*, Phillimore, 1986; *The History of the WGC Women's Luncheon Club 1929–1996*; C.V. Ivory: *Hatfield Hyde Gleanings and Memories*; Joan Long: *A First Class Job! – the story of Frank Murphy*, Joan Long, 1985; David Mander: *Images of Hertfordshire*, Sutton, 1998; *The Mud Chapel of Hatfield Hyde*, HH Primary School; Lionel L. Munby: *The Hertfordshire Landscape*, Hodder & Stoughton, 1977; Frederic J. Osborn: *Genesis of WGC – Some Jubilee Memories*, TPA, 1970; *Parkway (School) Memories 1934–84* ed. Kate Wentworth; Celia Reiss: *R.L. Reiss, a memoir, c. 1959*; Gwennah Robinson: *Hertfordshire – Barracuda guide to County History*, 1978; Maurice De Soissons: *WGC A Town Designed for Healthy Living*, CUP, 1988; Tony Rook: *A History of Hertfordshire*, Phillimore, 1997; Lisa Sheridan: *From Cabbages to Kings, an autobiography*, Odhams, 1955; *Stanborough School 1939–1989 Remembrance of (some) things past*; *The Time of our Lives 1939–1989* – WGC residents remember the Two World Wars; *Village Life in Hatfield Hyde* by 'RT'; Dora Ward: *Digswell From Domesday to Garden City*, WDRSA, 1953; A. Whittick: *FJO – Practical Idealist, a biography of Sir Frederick J. Osborn*, TCPA, 1987; *Welwyn Garden City*, WGC Company Ltd, 1930; *WGC Free Church 1921–71*; Welwyn Garden City News, 1921, 1924 ; *The WGC and Hatfield Pilot*, 1922; *Welwyn Times*, 1924, 1930, 1935, 1937, 1939, 1940, 1941, 1946, 1954; *Welwyn and Hatfield Times*, 1978; Anglo-American Industrial Newsletter, 1944; Window on the Past : Hertfordshire on film 1907–1959, Herts Library Service, 1989.